PICTURE FRAMING

as a business

J. Edwin Warkentin

1st WORLD
PUBLISHING

PICTURE FRAMING

as a Business

J. Edwin Warkentin

© J. Edwin Warkentin 2009

Published by 1stWorld Publishing
P. O. Box 2211, Fairfield, Iowa 52556
tel: 641-209-5000 • fax: 866-440-5234
web: www.1stworldpublishing.com

LCCN: 2008932326

SoftCover ISBN: 978-1-4218-9001-2

HardCover ISBN: 978-1-4218-9000-5

eBook ISBN: 978-1-4218-9002-9

This material has been written and published solely for educational purposes. The author and the publisher shall have neither liability or responsibility to any person or entity with respect to any loss, damage or injury caused or alleged to be caused directly or indirectly by the information contained in this book.

CONTENTS

CHAPTER FOUR

CHAPTER FIVE

CHAPTER SIX

CHAPTER SEVEN

CHAPTER EIGHT

CHAPTER NINE

CHAPTER TEN

CHAPTER ELEVEN

CHAPTER TWELVE

CHAPTER THIRTEEN

CHAPTER FOURTEEN

CHAPTER FIFTEEN

CHAPTER SIXTEEN

CHAPTER SEVENTEEN

CHAPTER EIGHTEEN

PREFACE

A great deal has been written on almost every aspect of picture framing, so it could be thought a bit cheeky for someone to actually write another book on the subject. However, after having given it serious thought, musing on my early years as a picture framer and my longing for help in those days, I have an emotional identification with today's framers, especially framers in remote communities. For picture framers, wherever they are located, there is a need for a reference publication such as this.

Several events brought about the writing of this book. First, the expressed need by my former students for reference material; second, my observation that many frame shop operators are short-changing themselves by confining their product line to the way things were "always done" in the past and yet, for one reason or another are not able to avail themselves of some formal instructions presented by either picture framers associations or a picture framers school; third, beginning framers who have no one to turn to for help or do not have seminars and workshops offered in their areas; and then lastly, after having operated two successful picture framing shops, founded two picture framing schools and published a magazine directed at the picture framing industry, I have some thoughts which I hope you will find beneficial.

This is not a book of rules, but rather a framework made up of ideas and suggestions to build up your business—a business well supplied with challenges, satisfaction, achievement and, dare I say it, profit.

The picture framing industry has been and is changing as new techniques are developed. The technology also changes as new computer-controlled equipment and other semi-automatic shop appliances become available and affordable. It is essential on practical grounds that picture framers keep up with these developments.

But that is not all. The custom framer, whether operating from a commercial location or is home-based, must learn how to run a business. Many skilled picture framers have had to close shop, not because the work was unsatisfactory, not because there were too few customers, but because either pricing was neglected, the books were not kept up to date, the inventory got out of hand or the necessity for advertising and promotion was disregarded. To cover all of those topics is a tall order, but we will have a "go" at most of them and my hope is that the reader will benefit—in fact, that is the purpose of this book.

—J. Edwin Warkentin, MA CPF

FOREWORD

It takes a lot of persistence and work, to start a picture framing shop. Early anticipation of owning your own business must be tempered with a realistic management plan to get the project off on a firm operational basis. This includes preparing the site for the frame shop, whether it is in a commercial setting or as a home-based business.

Organizing the site consist of many things such as the location—is it easily accessible for your customers, is it visible, is it compatible with the neighbourhood? Constructing the tables and other furnishings necessary for your enterprise requires planning and physical work. Once all the details have been worked out, or preferably before you start, you should ensure that you have enough funds available. Too many skilled framers have tried to start their own businesses without having given proper attention to their financial resources resulting in difficult times or complete failure.

Whether you are considering a home-based business or a store-front venture, do you have the necessary skills and self-discipline to set your business on the path for the success it deserves? If there is doubt regarding your proficiency, you might consider taking a course from one of the established picture framers schools. They teach you the physical aspects of operating a framing business but also business principles.

So, whether you start "from scratch" in your business or purchase an established business or a franchise; starting in your home or in a store-front location, remember, it is a business and your livelihood depends on its success. The challenge is exciting, the prospects are motivating, and the results are proof of your abilities.

ACKNOWLEDGEMENTS

The author of this publication credits a significant amount of its content to:

Columba Publishing

Crescent Cardboard

Fine Art Trade Guild, UK

Art Business Today

3M

Fletcher

Keencut

Morso

Phaedra

PPFA

Nielsen & Bainbridge

The author is indebted even more to former students, business associates who were willing to discuss their activities, and Patricia, my designated reviewer and wife.

INTRODUCTION

Where does one start if you know nothing about picture framing? Start by *looking*; looking unhurriedly and informally. Look at the pictures in your home, at the office, in your friends' homes, in galleries and museums. Look at the mats and frames on the artwork. Look at the framed needle-work and oil paintings. Get the "picture."

Mats on paper artwork are very important. Notice the colours and the textures, the wide borders and the narrow ones. Look closely at the mats that have decorative lines or panels and other embellishments. Look at the different types of frames. There are simple frames while others are in themselves ornate art. The balance of matting and frame is important. The functions of these framing components are to protect and enhance the artwork without detracting from it.

Picture framing is a craft. When learning a new skill it is advisable to start with something simple. Do a little at a time and work slowly. For your first framing project pick something manageable. Good picture framing is a matter of mastering techniques.

When you hang your first picture which you have framed yourself it will be with a feeling of pleasure and achievement. When a satisfactory point of practical skills has been attained, experiment a bit and look into the possibilities open to you which most subject matters can and might suggest.

Today there is a large swing toward having prints done on canvas by expensive printers. This equipment is essentially a printer that has been programmed to copy a print with archival grade inks through high resolution paint nozzles. This process permits an artist to have made as many copies as required. Each printed copy is in essence an original.

CHAPTER ONE

A Background History of Paper

It is common knowledge that paper is paper so why discuss its properties and characteristics? Well, paper does vary and these characteristics are very important to the preservation of art. Your customer's fine art deserves the maximum quality matting and mounting materials available today. So to carry out this commitment you are entitled to know the facts about the composition, characteristics and reliability of the mat boards you are using.

Because paper is cheap, readily available and expendable, it is often taken for granted. On the other hand, since paper is indispensable and poorly understood, there is a need for appreciating the effect of paper on art. Paper is such a familiar commodity in today's world that one seldom stops to reflect upon the materials that make newspapers, books, prints, certificates, napkins, cups, plates and countless other products.

The history of paper goes back to AD105 in China. Paper made from pulping plants, hemp and rags served as a less expensive, although less permanent alternative to silk fabric for writing and painting. Today, nearly two thousand years later, paper is still an unquestionable necessity in our daily lives. It is an inexpensive means for transmitting and preserving information, which includes pictures and prints. In China paper had other uses such as in the manufacturing of sliding screen partitions, fans and kites.

From China the technique of paper making spread to Korea, Japan and as international trade increased, to Egypt. From Egypt the practice of making paper spread swiftly throughout Europe and on to the New World.

The Japanese began making paper from the inner bark of the mulberry tree in the 7th century. Today, Japanese "rice paper" sold in art supply stores is made not from rice products but from mulberry bark. There are other trees developed by the Japanese people for producing highly refined acid-free paper similar to mulberry paper.

Europeans, at a much later date, used rags to manufacture paper, but the extensive use of bleach caused early deterioration of the paper and the supply of cotton and linen rags never caught up with the demand for paper. By 1800 substitutes were tried, such as asbestos, thistles, potatoes, leaves, corn husks, and cabbage stalks. Wood "paper" from wasp nests was tried with some success. Since then wood has come into its own for making paper.

Today newsprint and ground wood pulp are terms having a close association. Newsprint is weak because in its preparation procedure extremely short fibres are produced and much of the lignin, which, combined with cellulose molecules in the tree, is retained. Lignin when exposed to warmth and light, such as ultraviolet light, breaks down into acidic components which attack paper causing it to deteriorate. The wonder is that despite the use of these destructive agents by paper makers, any books or works of art on paper should have survived at all.

What can we learn from this information about paper? Most importantly, we must be discriminating regarding our use of paper. The paper we use must be suited for its purpose. If quality performance is required then quality materials must be chosen. Typical handmade paper, using cotton or linen fibres, from Europe or the Orient will answer the needs of specific users such as artists. Printing presses require a uniform thickness and weight with special sizing. The paper making industry has learned a great deal from the defective processes of the past and can now stipulate the chemical constituents of the paper pulp that modern technology can accommodate to extend the lifetime of their end-product. The ideal combination for paper permanence seems to be an acid free and alum free pulp made from the purest fibres possible, a condition that ironically was essentially fulfilled by ancient paper making methods, perhaps more by chance than design.

The purest paper making fibres available in quantity to the modern paper maker are new cotton fibres which contain no appreciable amounts of lignin. To help the external factors that affect permanence acid-free papers are made with a reserve of alkali present. The alkali acts as a buffer to neutralize any acid component present as a result of handling and exposure to the atmosphere. The pH scale, below, illustrates the relationship between acid and alkali components in paper products.

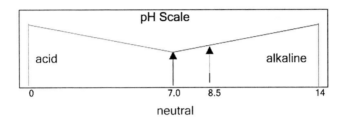

pH (German *Potenz* – power) and H(symbol for Hydrogen)), is a measure of acidity and alkalinity of a solution. Placed on a scale it varies from 0 (most acid) to 14 (most alkaline). It follows then that a pH of 7.0 indicates a neutral or balanced condition. In technical terms pH is the symbol indicating the negative logarithm of the hydrogen ion concentration in grams per litre of a solution. This is the same pH referred to when analysing the quality of air, soil or water. It is a critical measurement where it concerns paper and mat board manufacturing. Mat boards having a pH of 8.5 with an alkali reserve of 1 to 3 *per cent* are considered to be of conservation/archival/museum quality.

Mat Boards

Acid-free mat board, conservation/preservation board, museum board, archival board, rag board, and alpha cellulose board are all technical terms that have come into common usage in the picture framing industry. Even with all the current data available many of the terms are either misused or misunderstood. It is incumbent upon the picture framer, especially the one who claims to be a "conservation or preservation" framer, to be fully aware of the characteristics of the materials applied to a customer's treasure.

Rag Mat Board

Cotton seed   Cotton pod   Cotton boll

The term "rag" is a paper manufacturer's term going back to the 1400s when scraps of cotton rags were the main unrefined materials utilized in the production of paper. The term is still used to describe mat boards and paper produced from 100% new cotton pulp.

The cotton pulp used in the making of rag mat boards and other cotton paper products, are made from cotton linters. Cotton is planted and harvested annually. It is a yearly renewable resource having no impact effect on the country's forest assets. To compare, it requires 20 years or more to plant, grow and harvest a tree and then process it into cellulose pulp which then must be subjected to meticulous chemical modification to prepare it for use in the art industry.

Cotton is nature's perfect form of cellulose. Cotton pulp is 99% pure, lignin-free and also free from other non-cellulose impurities found in wood pulp. Cotton fibre pulp is stable, strong and of considerably higher quality than chemically bleached wood fibre pulp.

Paper products made of cotton fibre pulp, have a natural whiteness, and will not discolour over time. As well, cotton fibres do not require high levels of chemical bleaches, a necessary occurrence in making fine paper from wood fibre pulp.

Another feature of cotton fibres is that they intertwine resulting in a tenacious compliant mat board—more substantial than bleached wood fibre. Paper currency is made from rag fibre because of its toughness and resilience. Its capacity to stand up to extreme usage is due to the nature of the fibres and their configuration within paper.

Cotton linter pulp processing employs a small fraction of the destructive chemicals needed to manufacture alpha cellulose from wood pulp. Thus, the processing of pure cotton fibres results in a superior product and minor harm to the environment. Cotton fibre, as might be expected, is free of acids; there is no lignin, alum (utilized by some paper makers when using wood fibres) or other potentially harmful chemicals.

Purified Wood-based Mat Board

Cellulose fibres are the chief component parts of all plants, and are comprised of "chains" of sweet, crystalline carbohydrate molecules defined as alpha, beta, and gamma molecules. The alpha form of cellulose has the longest (softwood, 0.03937 to 0.24 inch, compared to cotton linters, which are 0.1 to 0.24 inch in length) and therefore the most stable chemical chain, resulting in the longest and strongest paper-making fibres.

In the last century wood pulp was processed by mechanical means. This meant that the wood was ground up, hence the term "ground wood pulp", including lignin, hemi-cellulose (a group of complex carbohydrates, for example, starch occurring mainly in plants) and other impurities, into pulp. Consequently the pulp, again referred to as ground wood, quickly deteriorated because of the lignin present. Mat boards made of this product are still used for projects where permanence is not an issue. However, for the preservation of art as in conservation framing, it is unsuitable.

To segregate the alpha cellulose essential for the production of high quality paper, the fibres go through a process of chemical and mechanical manipulation called "cooking" which dissolves the non-cellulose matter. The fibres are then washed to remove the unwanted ingredients, such as lignin, and bleached to purify the fibres even further. The water used in the washing procedure and in subsequent papermaking must be pure or purified which will leave minimal residual metals in the paper product. The type of sizing used in the manufacture of paper, as well as the adhesives employed in producing mat board, must accommodate alkali so as to neutralize any acid products present.

Regular (wood pulp) Mat Board

Wood pulp paper products are generally used in the manufacture of mat boards which must be buffered (neutralized), usually with calcium carbonate ($CaCO_3$) to suppress its natural acidic state. Although there are a number of factors that can have a degenerating effect on paper art, by far the worst of these is the highly acidic ground wood pulp used to make some of the lower quality mat and mounting boards.

Mat board that is manufactured with ground wood pulp will eventually absorb some of the acid due to air pollution, a humid environment which reacts with impurities in the mat board, human handling and lignin. Regular wood pulp contains lignin which when activated by exposure to heat, light or humidity becomes acidic. This acidic ingredient, in time, migrates on to the artwork resulting in "mat burn", a permanent yellow-brown discolouration around the window opening of the mat.

A widely used, and quite often misused, term in connection with regular mat board is "acid-free". The Library of Congress in the United States has published a work "Matting and Hinging of Works of Art on Paper" which states that the term acid-free does not necessarily mean that the material is top quality. In fact the publication declares, ". . . so-called acid-free mat board may be a product with an actual pH between 6 and 7." Mat boards made from wood pulp not having the lignin removed have a light cream coloured core. When this core is exposed by the bevel or V-groove to light containing the ultraviolet component, which is part of most light spectra, this core turns a beige colour before very long and eventually it changes to brown indicating that a chemical reaction has taken place and the pH has drifted to somewhere below 7.0 on the pH scale.

General

Here are a few other details about mat boards worth considering.

Colour – the colouring matter, whether it is dye or pigment, used in paper manufacturing must be both bleed proof and light fast. Climatic moisture may cause colours to run and exposure to light, notably ultraviolet light, may cause colours to fade. Both colour bleed and fade as applied to mat boards are not tolerated.

Squaring – before you make any attempt to square the mat board make sure that the cutter you use, whether it is wall mounted equipment or the squaring arm on your mat cutter, is square. To assume that the mat you have purchased is square can lead to wasted materials and frustration. Mat boards are manufactured slightly larger than 32" x 40" to compensate for possible shrinkage. Start with any side of the mat board and trim off roughly ¾". Continue this procedure until all four sides are done. A quick measurement of diagonal corners will tell you if the mat board is out of square. If the measurements are not the same it is off square.

Size – the thickness of mat boards varies as follows:

> 2-ply = 0.030"
> 4-ply = 0.055" (the most commonly used mat board thickness)
> 8-ply = 0.120"

The common sizes are 32" x 40" and 40" x 60" (referred to as oversize).

Storage – mat boards, being made of paper, readily absorb humidity. They should be stored in racks as far as possible from an outside wall. For storage purposes it is best to store them flat, however, in frame shops it is easier to locate and withdraw a mat board from a vertical rack than a horizontal rack. There is also less risk of damage if the boards are stored vertically.

Summary

The careful choice of matting materials is crucial to the proper care of art on paper. An awareness of the composition of these materials is imperative. Mat boards are manufactured in layers: a backing paper next to the art, a thicker core, and then a face paper on top of the mat. Mat boards vary in the make-up of the layers. Some have backing papers and cores that are considered to be of conservation standards but have face papers that are not. Frequently both the core and face paper are not of conservation quality.

The Library of Congress in association with Canadian Standards Agencies have defined explicit standards for durable mat boards:

- The pulp must be free from ground wood and lignin; must be of high content alpha cellulose, such as purified wood and cotton pulp.

- The finished mat board shall have a pH value between 7.2 and 9.5 with an alkali reserve between 3 and 5 per cent.

- Sizing that is inert or with a pH of 7+ should be used.

- No colour bleed must be evident when soaked in distilled water for 48 hours; no more than 5 points change in brightness must be evident after being exposed to 36 hours in a Fadeometer; the colouring medium used must be constant, non-bleeding and light-fast.

- Iron content must not exceed 30 parts per million and copper no more than 1PPM.

CHAPTER TWO

Shop Design

Available space can be viewed in various ways, such as flexibility, area assignment, the merchandise at hand, impact on marketing and production strategies.

Designing or redesigning a shop takes many skills. You need to be a merchant, designer, craftsman and organizer. Most beginner framers, through inexperience, make errors in shop layout and many experienced framers are too close or too busy to make major layout changes in their active shops.

Creating the correct work flow in your shop is of great importance to your production. The name of the game is production. You must produce to get paid. The production rate in your shop is a direct reflection of your organizational abilities as well as the types and condition of your equipment. Production will be improved with proper equipment in working condition and experienced employees. But no amount of new equipment and technology will make up for a lack of basic sense. A successful frame shop operation is a positive social and economic relationship between human beings, where both vendor and buyer benefit from the transaction. If you understand your customers and value their satisfaction, then technology may help you to succeed. If you neglect this basic requirement, then all the technology in the world is not likely to be of much use.

Before you start remodelling that space you have just leased or the garage next to your house for a framing shop, take time to think it through carefully. How much space will be needed for equipment and working space? How much of the business will be given to art and how much to framing? Have you divided the area properly? If you want your framing business to grow, have you made allowances for growth? Whether large or small, proper planning of your shop's specialties and needs is essential.

The space requirements for the different functions of a frame shop vary with:

- Size of space available.
- Kinds of products being developed and marketed.
- Types of framing being done.
- Space allotted to a picture gallery.

One way to approach this analysis is to identify the tasks you will be performing in your shop. Once you have identified the activity areas needed in your shop space, you can lay out the fixtures and equipment in the most efficient and cost effective way on a grid drawn to scale; the equipment and furnishings also drawn to scale and juggled around on the floor plan until you are satisfied with the locations. Taking time to plan, to build the necessary fixtures, and investing capital in good equipment, will in the long run make your business more profitable and more enjoyable.

For the shop that does custom framing, handles (framed or unframed) art, sells "frame related" craft articles, the space apportioned to each activity must reflect its priority with good judgment. Retail space is expensive so each section must "earn" its keep.

Then for the frame shop owner whose major activity is custom framing, that is, does it on the premises, careful consideration must be given to the shop space. The type and amount of equipment used will, to some degree, dictate how much working area will be needed. Something else that must be kept in mind is the efficient flow of the work from the time the item comes into the shop, where it is put initially, the process for completion and then where it is put for easy retrieval. There are ways to make the most of the space at hand. Of course, if active framing is not done at the location, more space is available for displaying and selling your products.

A rather poor shop layout or design can result in shoddy management, poor quality control, lost production, misuse of space, wasted steps, adverse working conditions, all resulting in inefficient employee production ending up with the loss of customers. A disorganized workshop implies incompetent management, means loss of production expressing itself in never knowing where anything is, to being totally unaware where you placed the item to be worked on next.

For wall covering in your display (gallery) area you might consider carpeting it. Carpet is a functional alternative to painted or panelled walls. Not only does it give an atmosphere of quietness but it also covers nail holes created when hanging art. Another contemporary alternative is using slot wall panels. They look clean with minimum maintenance.

The businesslike workshop means greater time for marketing and planning, punctual order turn around, greater number of orders, research on and procuring additional efficient equipment and fewer errors. The equipment and supplies organization in the workshop design is important for efficient and sensible traffic flow through the production area.

It might appear obvious, but it bears emphasizing, that the mat boards should be in proximity of the mat cutting table,. Accommodation should also be provided for storage of small, yet usable, mat board pieces. Glass should be stored near the glass cutter and away from the assembling table to prevent accidents to the artwork—accidents such as glass cleaner spray, possibly broken glass and tiny shards damaging the mat and the art. Again, at the risk of sounding patronizing, mouldings should be stored near the cutting machines; this includes containers for short pieces. The best design is one which follows the framing project in a logical, progressive pattern throughout the shop, ending up in the OUT storage area for customer pick-up.

Many frame shops have what are customarily referred to as "clean" and "dirty" areas, isolated from each other by as much as space permits. The "clean" section is where the art itself is handled and where mat cutting is done. The "dirty"—perhaps dusty is a better word, is the section for cutting moulding and glass, cleaning glass, applying spray adhesives and other contaminants such as lacquers or toxic materials that might be present. In fact if spraying of any kind is necessary, a spray booth exhausted to the outdoors will prove to be not only beneficial but required by the health authorities.

Practical Workshop and its Equipment

(Note: for conversion to metric measurements see Glossary - Metric Conversion.)

Work Table

Among the important pieces of furnishings in a picture framing shop is the assembly or fitting table, where frames are put together and the whole project is completed. The arrangement for this table would preferably be an "island" table you can walk around, located in the workshop area. It should be as large as space permits. The table top material may be plywood or particle board anywhere from ¾" up to 1¼" thick. The size will depend on how much space is available, but 4' x 8' is first-rate.

The working height of the worktable is critical, since this decides whether you will be comfortable working at it or develop a chronically aching back. One way to determine the correct height for you, bend over at the waist so that your back is parallel with the floor. Measure the distance from your shoulder to the floor. This is the height for your work table, and will be between 33 inches and 39 inches. Although this appears to be a bit on the high side, it proves in practice to be quite comfortable. Make sure that the construction is solid with enough braces to prevent the table from shifting. The table could be covered with either vinyl linoleum or low-pile carpeting. It is also a good idea to recess the mat cutter into one end of the table so that the table is at the same level as the top of the mat cutter, allowing the mat board to lie flat at all times. Drawers and shelves under the table are useful.

Mat Cutter

The most-used piece of equip-ment in the frame shop is the mat cutter. You can do without a chopper or saw by having your frames "chopped." You can do without an under-pinner by having your wood frames "joined." You can do without a dry mount press or vacuum press by using alternative methods of mounting artwork; but the mat cutter is indispensable. Mat cutters vary in length from 24 inches to 60 inches. The mat cutter, as has been noted, should be placed at the end of the work table and preferably recessed. This will permit access to the cutter whether cutting left—or right-handed. It will also allow the squaring arm to be supported by the table top.

Wall Mounted Glass/Cardboard Cutter

After the straight line mat cutter, the most useful piece of equipment is the wall mounted glass, cardboard and acrylic cutter. This unit is usually fastened to a solid wall and requires no more floor space than the depth of it, approximately 18 inches.

Oval/Circle Cutter

Although most mats will be cut with a straight line mat cutter, oval and circle openings add another pleasing dimension to the picture framer's stock of techniques. There are several models available, from the portable kind that can

be stored in a drawer or on a shelf, to the more heavy-duty type that requires dedicated table space because of its weight and size. The latter type can also cut glass ovals and circles.

Mounting Press

Whether the framing shop uses a vacuum press or a dry mount press, they both require assigned table space, and therefore floor space. The dry mount press is possibly the most versatile since it can handle over-size mounting projects; it is fast and can do laminating with great efficiency. The vacuum press, on the other hand, does not require warm-up or cool down times, and the adhesive materials used are considerably less expensive. It does have size limitations — limited to the size of the press. Heated vacuum presses are also available.

Moulding Cutting Equipment

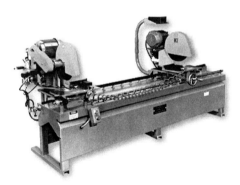

The two pieces of equipment used to cut moulding are saws and choppers. If a saw is used it is advisable to get a double mitre saw with dust collecting capability. One of the major irritations in the frame shop is dust. Some saws are made to cut both wood and metal. The chopper is limited to cutting wood but it has the advantage of being both dust and noise free.

Lateral space and supports must be available to accommodate mouldings 12 feet in length. Storage racks should be constructed in close proximity to the cutting machine. Storage for surplus pieces of moulding must be provided.

Summary

There is no one pattern for a frame shop layout that fits all spaces; but some points worth considering as they apply to most locations are:

- Provide ample storage space for mat boards and glass, located close to the cutters.

- Provide ample storage racks for moulding inventory.

- If possible, locate the main work table near the centre of the shop.

- Allocate equipment and work table space to the greatest time saving advantage.

- Provide lots of storage space.

- Take time to plan, to build the necessary fixtures, and investing capital in good equipment, this will in the long run make your business more profitable and enjoyable.

- If active framing is not done at the shop location, more space is available for displaying and selling your products.

- The production rate in your shop is a direct reflection of your organizational abilities and the amount and condition of your equipment.

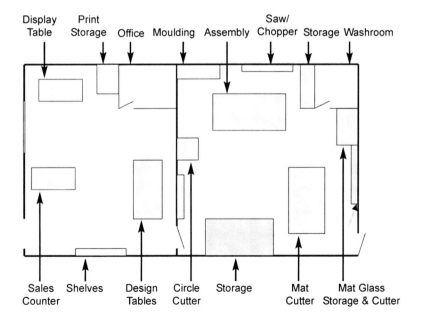

This workshop area of 753.5 sq. ft. accommodates the workshop, its furnishings, equipment and washroom.

Safety Tips

When it comes to working with power equipment, sharp hand tools, paints and chemicals, glass and electrical appliances, caution and common sense are the principles to keep in mind. This applies equally to the novice and the experienced artisan. The following suggestions come as a result of operating a frame shop with its potential disasters:

- Be careful when handling mat cutter blades. Most mat cutters have a warning label on the cutter head, and for good reason. Rather than depositing used blades in the garbage they might be stored in a covered tin and disposed of when full.

- Chopper and saw blades, drill and router bits, as well as knife blades must be kept clean and sharp. Dull tools are dangerous, not only to the worker but also to the material being worked on.

- Use ear protectors when operating noisy power tools. The high frequencies produced by these machines can damage your ears—permanently.

- If you must remove the guard on your table saw to cut through a high profile moulding. Replace it immediately when done and leave it in place for other work. A careless or "take-a-chance" disposition, results in a diminishing finger inventory.

- Wear rubber or chemical proof gloves when handling solvents or other chemicals; many of them can cause skin injury.

- Wear gloves when handling glass, especially large sheets. The sharp edges and corners can result in severe injuries if mishandled. Special glass handling gloves are available.

- Keep the working area neat and tidy. When you are finished with materials and tools, put them away; clutter leads to disorder and accidents.

- Chemicals, such as adhesives, spray paints, varnishes, thinners, solvents and cleaners should be used and stored in a well-ventilated area. Even so, to be on the safe side wear a gas mask when using chemicals.

Fumes given off by some of these chemicals are toxic and others are extremely flammable.

- Disconnect, by pulling the power cord, electrical equipment, such as saws, before changing blades or bits. Unplug power equipment or "trip" the circuit breakers before leaving at the end of the work day. Check power cords and extension cords for wear.

- Be sure you wear a dust mask and goggles when working with abrasives, such as in glass etching. The mask is also advisable in dusty areas. Goggles should be worn when cutting moulding to prevent metal or wood particles from damaging your eyes.

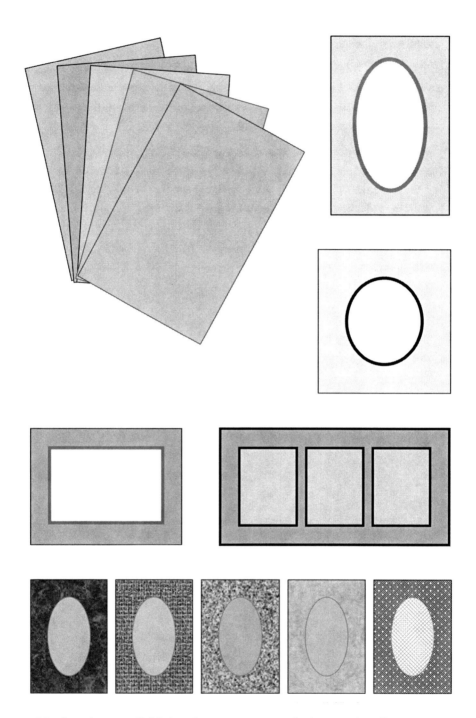

Mat boards are available in a large assortment of colours and surface.textures.

CHAPTER THREE

Mats and Mat Cutting

When designing a mat and frame combination for a piece of art the objective is to fashion a setting that enriches without compromise. It is important that the design in framing a picture motivates the viewer to look at the artwork rather than the framing.

Matting, more than any other area of picture frame design, is the gauge by which the abilities of the creative picture framer are measured. Of all the skills required of the custom framer, none is as rewarding as that of mat cutting. Although mats continue to serve a protective function their artistic role has developed into something of equal importance in the overall framing design.

The ordinary mat is no longer "ordinary." No longer do plain white mats satisfy every framing job. Today's mats are made of paper, cloth and glass; they are enhanced with paint, ribbons, gold leaf, carvings and, of course, more mats. Techniques and designs which the framer has developed for customers will have a stamp of character that is distinctive. The picture framer must be prepared to sell creative matting to the customer. The more skilful he or she is the more ingenious the marketing method must be.

Mat Logic

- There are several reasons for using mats in a framing project. They vary from being attractive to being practical.
- Mats intensify the picture by highlighting certain colours or the picture's intent.
- Mats have the ability to focus the observer's attention into the picture itself as well as providing separation between the picture, the frame and its setting.
- Mats provide the needed separation between artwork and glass. This separation is necessary to prevent condensation which can form behind the glass, from coming in contact with the art.
- Mats provide a substructure for decorations and carved openings for further enhancement of the art.
- Mats, from a purely mercenary point of view, pay off.

Proportions

Proportion is something seen rather than measured. It is a visual balance of colour, texture, light and shapes. When deciding how wide the mat borders should be, creating a pleasing appearance is the only rule. If the matting looks suitable then in all likelihood it is correct. There are, however, some ideas about matting that are worth bearing in mind.

- Small, narrow mats tend to distract the eye with too many patterns or lines.
- Mats on small pictures should be wide to emphasize the picture.
- Most popular mat styles for small or modern artworks use equal border sizes. However, uniform border widths on large pictures are generally modified by placing a wider ("weighted") bottom border, from ¼" to 1." This is intended to correct a visual aberration, which makes the bottom appear narrower than the other sides when the framed art is viewed at above eye level.
- Long, narrow artwork as a rule looks better with both the top and bottom mat widths made wider than the two sides.

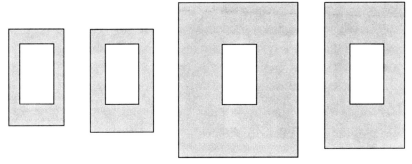

These mats have the same size openings.

These prints are all the same size.

The relationship between artwork and where it will hang is important. The customer should be asked about the intended location especially if the intention is to hang a simple, primitive painting on a busy wallpapered wall, you will need to select framing materials that will give the artwork "space." No matter what you are framing—a shoe, an original pen and ink drawing, a coin, or a certificate, each piece has a design that should be enhanced by the framing.

The skills which you will acquire with practice include artistic and practical in the course of selecting and cutting the mat (and moulding). Basic skills are necessary but picking the mat (and moulding) materials, is entirely a decision of individual taste. Everyone has his or her own concepts and reactions regarding pictures and how they should be framed. There are no definite rules. If it appeals to the owner of the artwork it is a success.

Pictures are framed to give them a finished look and for protection. But no matter how elegant or expensive the framing materials might be it is impossible to make a poor picture look good. Furthermore, the framing components should complement the picture, enriching it, but not competing. Select your materials to agree with the theme.

When a satisfactory point of practical skill has been attained, experiment a bit and look into the possibilities open to you which most subject matters can and might suggest.

Summary

- Avoid matting with a colour that is not in the picture.
- Where it is possible, refrain from matting in black and white. A white mat board inclines to make white areas in the picture appear off white or creamy.
- An off-white mat brings out the pristine whites in the picture. Similarly, a black mat tends to make black parts of the picture appear grey, so it is better to choose a grey mat thereby emphasizing the black areas of the picture.
- Too narrow mat borders tend to compress the artwork.
- You might consider weighting the bottom border to produce a pleasing visual equilibrium to the mat, although at the present time the most popular mat styles use equal border widths on all sides.

Mat Cutting

The artwork you are framing might take up the entire piece of paper on which it is printed; that is, the image extends out to all four sides of the paper as with papyrus art and watercolours, or it may be positioned in the centre with a margin of blank paper around it.

If the image covers the entire sheet of paper there are two ways to mat it. One way is to mount it on to a coloured mat board, cutting the window opening on the top mat larger than the image, thereby permitting the viewer to see the mounting board around the print as well as the edges of the picture (Option A below). This is especially attractive if the outside of the picture has a decorative or ragged edge such as handmade paper and papyrus.

Option A

Image to be matted.   Two mats joined   Image matted and framed
Figure 1   Figure 2   Figure 3

The other way, and by far the most general, is to cut the window opening slightly smaller than the image (Option B, below). What this means is that the mat will cover or "crop" part of the picture—as little as possible, usually 1/8" on each side (Fig.4, next page). If the picture image is 8" X 10" the window opening would then be 7¾" X 9¾".

Fig. 1 shows a print 8" X 10" without a border. We will crop or cover 1/8" of the print on each side. Now it becomes 8-(1/8"+1/8") = 7¾" and 10-(1/8"+1/8") = 9¾", or 7¾" X 9¾" dimensions of the mat window opening. What we have to do now is determine how wide the mat border will be. It is common, but by no means obligatory unless the customer demands it, to make the bottom border a little wider than the top and sides. In our example we will make the top and sides 2" and the bottom 2½" in width.

Once we have all the figures in place we calculate the dimensions of our matting project, Fig. 2, which will tell us the outside dimensions of the mat board—11¾"(7¾ +2 +2) x14¼"(9¾ + 2 + 2½). Incidentally, this is also the size of the glass and the frame. Fig. 3 shows the matted and framed print. Once we have cut the mat to the right size, 11¾"x14¼", it now remains to cut the opening.

Option B

Fig.1 - print

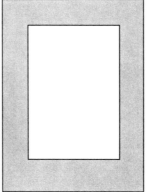

Fig. 2 - mat with a 2" border

Fig.3 - matted print

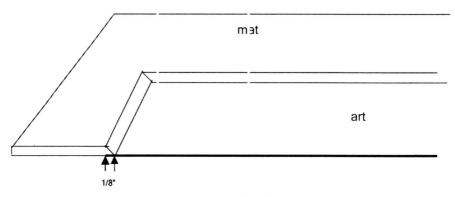

Fig. 4

You should *not* cut the mat opening (window) to the exact size as the outer dimensions of the borderless print. Paper expands and contracts with temperature and humidity changes resulting in buckling at the edge of the mat opening. When framing original or limited edition pictorial art it is a standard practice to leave ½" of the border (generally white) showing at the top and sides of the image and slightly more at the bottom to accommodate the artist's signature and any other details of the image such as the edition number and title.

Typical Image Size	Suggested Mat Border Width (inches)
5x7	1 to 1½
8x10	1½ to 2
11x14	2 to 2½
16x20	2½ to 3
20x24	3 to 4

Before you do anything in preparing your artwork for framing it is essential that you complete a procedure to accurately measure the image you want to display. All other components of the project are based on these precise measurements.

Added to this image size are the border dimensions in order to ascertain the frame size. It does not really matter if you have a frame custom-made, ready-made or cut and join it yourself and whether or not you mount and mat the artwork, the size and shape of the image to be shown in that frame is the first set of figures needed.

Cutting a single mat - (Metric—see Glossary)

Consult the operating directions for your mat cutter.

Referring back to the **Option B Figs. 1, 2, 3** examples, let's go through the procedure for cutting a mat.

1. With reference to Fig.1, above, we see the image is 8"x10" and extends to the edge of the paper. The mat will cover (crop) 1/8" on each side making it now 7¾" x 9¾".

2. The mat will have 2" borders on the sides and top with 2½" on the bottom.

3. Fig. 3 shows the print matted.

4. Calculate the outside dimensions of the mat:

   width: 7¾" + 2 + 2 = 11¾"

   length: 9¾" + 2 + 2½ = 14¼" - Fig.2.

5. Cut the mat board to size.

6. Place the mat cutter guide bar to 2".

7. Place the mat board from 5 above **face down** under the *cutting bar*.

8. Using a <u>pencil</u> mark both sides and top—Figure A (below).

9. Place the guide bar at 2½. Mark the fourth side with a pencil.

10. Cut this fourth side.

11. Finish cutting the other three borders. Figure B (below).

12. Figure C (below) shows the finished mat.

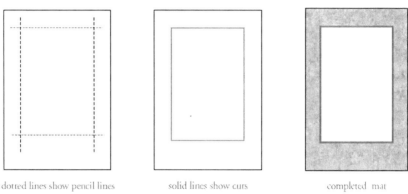

dotted lines show pencil lines   solid lines show cuts   completed mat

Fig. A -reverse side of mat   Fig. B – mat cut (reverse side)   Fig. C – (front side)

Cutting a Double Mat

Cutting a double mat is without a doubt one of the first procedures that a custom framer must master, after becoming proficient at producing a single mat. The artistic qualities of multiple matting permit the framer to enrich the customer's art. Inserting mats of contrasting or harmonizing colours and colours that bring out an obscure item in the picture through a second or third mat is a customary method of enhancement. Multiple mats also have the ability to "funnel" the observer's visual attention. To sum up, three-quarters of picture framing jobs require the custom framer to be skilled at cutting multiple mats—mostly double mats.

back of top mat showing the
adhesive strips

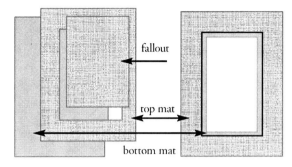

double mat

1. Select a mat board 8" X 10" — this is A, the top mat.

2. Cut a second mat 7¾" X 9¾" — this is B, the bottom mat.

3. Measure, mark and cut a 1¾" border in A - face down; attach B to A, face down, with adhesive strips. The reason for cutting B smaller than A is to ensure that the edges of B will not interfere with the measuring and cutting for the window area

4. Temporarily replace the fallout in A with adhesive strips.

5. Measure, mark and cut a 2" border in B, again, face down.

A painted bevel is very effective. Some customers do not like the white bevel. It should take no longer than 10 minutes and the going charge is $12.00 for any size mat.

CHAPTER FOUR

Understanding Colour

When we stop to think about what colour means to us in our everyday lives, it is hard to imagine what a colourless world would be like. It would be dull and lifeless. Colour adds excitement and intrigue to our sense of sight. We are delighted by the lively colours in paintings by any of the Group of Seven or the autumn beauty of a forest. Science has confirmed that colour affects our emotions. Hot colours such as reds and yellows, cool blues and peaceful greens stir up different responses in people. But, what is colour? How do we see it? How is it reproduced?

Colour is a complicated subject. It may be studied in great depth. In fact, there are university degree programs available in colour science. In this section we will attempt to simplify the subject of colour and provide an understanding of basic colour principles.

What is Colour?

It is hard to picture a world absent of colour—but that is what really exists. All the objects that surround us have no colour. Colour exists only in our minds. Colour is a visual perception that includes three elements —a light source, an object and a viewer. Light from the sun or another light source strikes objects around us, is reflected and modified by the objects, then reaches the receptors in our eyes and is interpreted by our brains into something we call colour. Since colour only exists in our minds, explaining the physical aspects of colour is just part of the story.

The way objects appear to us and the judgments we make about colour are determined by a combination of many factors. Some of these factors are easy to measure while others are not. Individual perceptual differences, eye fatigue and mood of the viewer are as important to a discussion about colour as are the properties of light sources and objects. Colour as perceived by the human eye cannot be simulated by any instrument, nor can it be reproduced by any printing process.

Light is essential for vision. Light causes colour. Without light, colour would not exist. Light that appears white to us, such as light from the sun, is actually composed of many colours. Each colour has its own measurable wavelength or combination of wavelengths. (Light travels in waves much like waves produced by dropping a pebble in a pond, except light waves are extremely small.) Wavelengths of light are not coloured, but produce the *sensation* of colour. Light is a form of energy. All wavelengths of light are part of electromagnetic energy. The spectrum is a continuous sequence of energy waves that vary in length from short to long. Visible light—wavelengths our eyes can detect, is a small portion of the entire spectrum. At one end of the visible spectrum are short wavelengths of light we perceive as violet. At the other end of the visible spectrum are longer wavelengths of light we perceive as red. All other colours we can see in nature are found somewhere along the spectrum between violet and red. Beyond the limits at each end of the visible spectrum are short wavelengths of ultraviolet light and X-rays and long wavelengths of infrared radiation and radio waves which are not visible to the human eye.

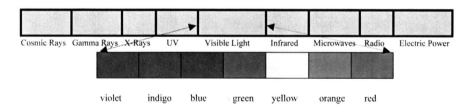

We can separate a beam of white light into its component colours by passing it through a glass prism which causes the light beam to bend. Each wavelength, or colour, bends at a slightly different angle which separates white light into an array of colours. When the sun comes out after a rainstorm, water droplets in the air can act as prisms and display the arc of colours in the sky we see as a rainbow.

J. Edwin Warkentin

White light Refracted Through a Prism

In 1676, Sir Isaac Newton found that white light, when passed through a prism, disperses into different, distinct colours that oscillate at dissimilar rates. By bending this stream of colours into a circle, Newton produced the first *colour wheel.*

If the visible portion of the spectrum is divided into thirds, the predominant colours are *blue, green and red.* These are the <u>primary colours of light.</u> Visible colours can be arranged in a circle, commonly known as the **colour wheel.** Blue, yellow, and red form a triangle on the colour wheel. In between these primary colours are the secondary colours, green, orange and violet which form another triangle. Colours opposite each other on the colour wheel represent complementary colours.

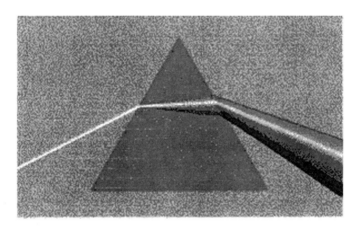

Refraction of light through a prism

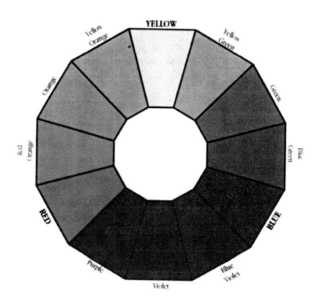

Colour Wheel

Colour Power

Colour informs, it communicates. Colour conveys statements about mood, can express lifestyle (sense of values) can raise or lower blood pressure, wear you down, or revitalize you. In a subliminal way colours may be categorized as follows:

RED—excites; it increases body temperature and accelerates the heart beat.

ORANGE—provokes; indicates a lack of sensitivity to other people's views.

YELLOW—alerts; it demands attention and causes anxiety and wariness.

GREEN—calms; it suggests tranquillity, freshness and renewal.

BLUE—anticipates; this is a colour of expectation, stability and esteem.

VIOLET—prestigious; a colour of dignity and passion.

GREY—rational; this is a colour showing intelligence, wisdom, elegance, and distinction.

Everyone notices a lady in red. Red cars get more speeding tickets. When you see red, your blood sugar soars, your heart speeds up, you breathe faster, your blood pressure goes up and your muscles tense.

Colour actually triggers hormonal, chemical reactions in all of us, regardless of age, gender, upbringing—or even colour-blindness.

Taste and training affect the way we think about colour, but everyone's impression is based on a physical response to colour—in advertising, in retailing, in job interviews.

Fire fighters, police on the beat, your banker, your lawyer and the heads of governments should wear dark blue, which implies authority and responsibility, yet is friendly. Brown is powerless; mid-tone green elicits a negative response, black is aloof.

Proctor & Gamble packages Tide detergent in its signature box because orange suggests power, and blue and white together say cleanliness and purity.

Yellow causes babies to cry and makes grown-ups cranky.

If you want a business lunch to be brief, eat in a restaurant where the decor is bright yellow and red. For somewhat longer discussions, select a restaurant with some lighter reds—peach or apricot—with dark green accents. For leisurely meals, go to restaurants that use burgundies and maroons, which cause people to lose track of time.

For retailing, a store's sign and façade must wear colours that inspire a positive response. Customers decide in 90 seconds whether a store is appealing or not, so look at your store from a customer's point of view.

The best exterior colours are those that help position you favourably in the customer's mind. Up-scale customers respond well to muted, neutral colours and to dark colours such as burgundy, hunter green, and navy. Lower income customers prefer bright colours. Men respond favourably to yellow-based reds, blues, browns, greens and blacks, and they prefer strong undiluted colours. Women are drawn to blue-based reds and tinted colours —those colours that are toned down with white.

What works for your customers? Visit stores that sell goods and services to your potential customer and find out!

For my frame shop I rented a building that had been a bank. I noticed that one of the rooms was painted a bright yellow. Upon asking the former tenant the reason for the irritating colour he said it had been the lunch room where his employees spent longer than the fixed time, prior to having it painted yellow, after which they spent as little time as possible in the room, translating into more production time.

Select Colour for Picture Framing Projects

The picking of a colour for the mat is almost totally subjective. It is personal. To assist the framer in making the right choices, a couple of suggestions might help. One is the colour's visual weight, or value, that is, its lightness or darkness in relation to black and white. Another point is that of being able to identify the dominant, neutral and prominent colours in the artwork and then to select mats that will enhance the art.

Colour Value

HUE + WHITE = TINT

HUE + GREY = TONE

HUE + BLACK = SHADE

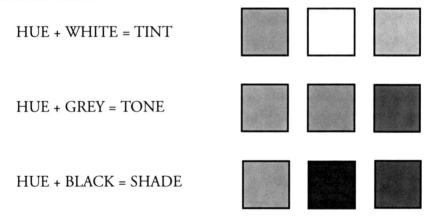

J. Edwin Warkentin

This illustrates the same picture with three different mat colour backgrounds.

As professional workers, when we propose the best imaginable mat and framing choices to our customers and then let them decide what best satisfies their expectations, we have succeeded. As the illustrations on the previous page show, there is not just one combination of mats that might do justice to the picture, but the unacceptable combination is the one the customer dislikes.

The framing design must present a complete visual continuous flow between art and framing materials applied so that the artwork is enhanced by the colours encompassing it. You must be careful not to overdo the framing part so as to not eclipse the subject. If you, as the professional frame designer understand the art accurately, it should remain to be the principal visual element, even after it is framed.

How do you ensure that the artwork appears at its best advantage and yet keeps the customer satisfied? To satisfy both conditions, you must be sensitive to the colour needs of the customer and allow expectations of what is good for the art.

In the case of a double mat, the inner or bottom mat, often referred to as a fillet, draws attention to some particular aspect in the artwork. For the observer, it also satisfies symmetry with the frame. The top mat on the other hand, provides the necessary function of tying the project together by supplying the striking delicate or dark characteristics in the artwork.

Summary

The problem of selecting colour designs for mats is one that picture framers are faced with every day. With the continual arrival of new mat board colours and the task of choosing the right colours for customers repeatedly demanding more colour choices, it is the framer, familiar with today's colours, who can readily gain the confidence and loyalty of clients and increase sales at the design counter.

White, grey and black, although frequently referred to as "colours", are actually lacking colour. They are not found on the colour wheel, but their importance lies in that they are used to create tints, tones and shades.

We have found that by adding white, grey or black to a colour we achieve tints, tones or shades, respectively, of that colour. White, grey and black are considered neutral colours; in fact, grey is frequently used as a "compromise" when nothing else seems to fit.

Choosing appropriate colours to present a piece of art work:

- Look at the piece thoroughly; note the colours that are most conspicuous; which colour covers the most area and which the least. Mats and frames can replicate the same   proportions of colours, for example, a winter scene with large amounts of white and accents of green and grey, might have a white mat or a green/grey frame.

- Attempt to duplicate the art in the framing of it. Is the art physically large, medium or small? Is the texture smooth, rough, heavy or thick? Are the lines bold, delicate, round or straight? Is the colour opaque, transparent, pale, bright or dull?

- Consider the place where the art work will hang; the wall colour; the furniture design; the room décor.

- Colour surface paper of mat boards are developed from pigments and dyes; pigments are substances that impart colour to animal or vegetable tissues. Dyes are classes of finely powdered, insoluble matters.

Ironically, colour may not be the framer's first topic of discussion with clients. They are happy to talk size, type of moulding and cost, but faced with hundreds of mat choices, they may find colour an unmanageable subject.

CHAPTER FIVE

Moulding and Frames

A frame is the final step in the creation, portraying the artwork and setting it off from the surroundings, of a painting or drawing. The frame is a separation that keeps the viewer's attention on the art instead of wandering across the wall where it is displayed. The frame underscores the whole matter of symmetry which embodies the relationship between the illustrated elements and the picture's boundaries. Customers depend on the expertise of the professional framer to complete that final step.

In addition to this artistic function, a frame protects the art from physical damage and deterioration. Works of art on paper are especially open to all kinds of damage from handling, dust and moisture, tiny insects, mould and atmospheric pollutants.

Wood Moulding

Picture frames manufactured from wood moulding are, and have been for ages, in greater demand than those made from metal, although the gap is narrowing. It is to the picture framer's advantage to have knowledge and understanding of the types of woods used and their finishes.

Wood is divided into two main classifications, hardwoods and softwoods; hardwoods being of the deciduous variety and softwoods from coniferous trees such as evergreens. But in lumber jargon hardwood and softwood refer to the ease or difficulty which it presents for "working."

Some of the common varieties of wood used in picture moulding are:

basswood (linden tree) – this wood is light in colour, the grain is not distinct but straight, easily shaped, takes glue readily, does not split easily when nailed, is permeable so requires several sealer coats. It is regarded as one of the finest woods for picture frame moulding.

poplar – this wood is straight-grained, fairly hard wood of a light colour, the grain, although hardly noticeable, is straight, it may be sanded to a very fine finish and takes paint readily, stain and gold leaf. Because of these features, poplar is considered a very fine wood for picture frame moulding.

ramin – a hardwood tree, indigenous to South-East Asia, which produces a medium hardwood lumber and because of its pale, plain, smooth, regular straight-grained structure can be finished in almost any medium. The characteristics of ramin, along with the ease with which it can be worked, make it a desirable wood for picture frame moulding.

oak – is a readily available hardwood which is heavy and has a characteristic grain. It can be stained or presented in its natural yellow brown or grey brown colour. If the wood is not milled carefully, the moulding tends to warp. This is one of the most popular woods for picture frame moulding.

pine – a soft, white or light yellow wood, uniformly grained, resistant to twisting and lightweight, is used extensively, because of these properties, for picture frames and stretcher bars. Pine is capable of being easily shaped or carved to form the intricate profiles of some mouldings.

birch – similar to poplar in that it is a semi-hardwood, has little noticeable grain, is light in colour—yellow-brown, and in lengths of moulding, straight. Although the wood is hard and dense it is readily shaped.

There are other woods, exotic woods, such as maple, chestnut, ash, mahogany, cherry, walnut, teak and various other imported types included in picture frame moulding. The trend has been to fill a wall in the framing gallery with many corner samples. Customers have come to expect this. The truth of the matter is that 10% to 20% of the samples displayed provide for 90% of frames sold. Some independent-minded shop owners have limited their wood moulding samples to six or eight. One of the responsibilities of moulding suppliers is to advise the framing gallery manager and give guidance as to which mouldings will sell. This takes much of the speculative component out of the business. In the final analysis, the mouldings you choose to display can make the difference in the rate of growth in your framing business. There are literally hundreds of profiles available. Among the common types are the following:

Length — Chop — Open Frames

Length means ordering moulding footage or "sticks" for stocking the framing shop. Fifty feet of moulding should produce from 6 to 8 frames. Distributors offer price breaks depending on the amount you buy. Buy only what you think you can use in the immediate future. Stocking moulding requires space and money—both rare commodities. Get a well-rounded selection in finishes, profiles and quality. Remember waste, about 20%, must be factored into the order. In other words, if the frame is 16" X 20", the amount of moulding required is: (16 + 16 + 20 + 20) X 1.20 = **86.4" or 7.2 feet.** The supplier will, in all probability not have that exact size in stock, so you might get 8 feet, 10 feet or even 12 feet. Now you have to consider what will be done with the extra pieces, after all you have paid for them.

Chop Service offered by most moulding distributors, means that you give them your frame size measurements and you get four pieces cut to size. This is a viable option if you:

- want to try a certain profile.
- want to avoid waste, noise, dust.

- do not have the space for moulding inventory or a room for the cutting equipment.
- do not have the capital to invest in equipment or moulding stock.
- want to have a large selection of corner samples without stocking inventory.
- want to put your time into more productive things in your shop.

Another problem which occurs occasionally is that a stick of moulding comes to your shop in a twisted or bent condition and frequently with imperfections such as knots which are difficult to cut around. You should return mouldings with these imperfections, which take time and possibly delays to complete the order you had promised your customer for a certain date. Although human errors creep into chop orders as well, it is highly unlikely that you will receive a marred set of mouldings.

The cost difference between length moulding and chop is about 40%. What this means is that a moulding with a base price of:

$2.61 per foot in length would cost 2.61 X 1.4 or $3.65 per foot chopped to size.

The 16" X 20" frame would cost you: $2.61 X 7.2' = **$18.79 in length,** without considering the waste piece left over from a stick 8', 10' or 12' in length, also at $2.61 a foot. The chop service would be: $3.65 X 7.2' = **$26.31.**

Open Frame a service providing the framer with a fully cut and joined picture frame with the following features:
- You have a complete frame—no cutting, joining, or touching up.
- There is no need to have expensive cutting and joining equipment or inventory.
- It facilitates production runs.
- You have frame products if your framer is sick or on vacation.
- You have frames even if your location is in a mall where space is limited and noise and dust are prohibited.

The cost difference between length moulding and an open frame approximates 60%. So in the above example of a completed frame 16" X 20" would cost: <u>($2.61 X 1.60) X 7.2 = **$30.07**</u> or $11.28 more than a length production, ignoring the pieces left over from the supplied stick.

To summarize the cost difference for a wood frame 16" X 20" at a base price of $2.61 per foot:

Length moulding—$2.61 X 7.2(feet) = $18.79 (**not considering waste**)

Chop service—$2.61 X 1.4 X 7.2 = 26.31 (**no waste, no saw, minimal labour**)

Open frame—$2.61 X 1.6 X 7.2 = 30.07 (**no waste, no saw, no labour**)

Making the Frame

The first thing that must be done before the moulding is cut is to select and inspect it for defects. The moulding is then measured, cut and joined, followed by touch up if necessary.

Selection involves choosing the appropriate profile, ensuring that it is straight and no flaws present. To discover flaws once the frame is assembled can be time consuming and costly; taking a frame apart risks damaging it.

Measurement makes certain that the moulding is long enough. As with cutting mats, it is prudent to measure twice and cut once. The length of the moulding required is the perimeter of the item to be framed plus 20%

The Saw

Cutting and mitring can be done with a hand saw and mitre box, an electric saw or chopper. Whichever method is used, the cuts must be clean, smooth and accurate. Electric mitre saws, the cut-off type that swivel at least from +45° to -45°, are perhaps the most versatile moulding cutting tools in the frame shop because they will cut wood as well as soft metals. They are also useful for sawing the angles necessary for hexagon and octagon frames. The double mitre saw, comprising two saw blades permanently set at 90° to each other, cuts two adjacent angles of the frame concurrently. The blades are enclosed which is a desirable safety factor.

Ten-inch blades having 80 to 100 carbide tipped teeth, alternately bevelled, are in common use. On this blade, every tooth is bevelled at a 15° angle, with every fifth tooth cut straight as a raker to clean out the cut and make it smooth.

The Chopper

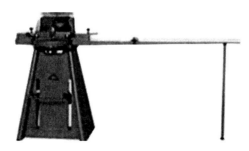

The chopper force-cuts through wood moulding. It has two heavy, extremely sharp blades set at right angles to each other which are manually or pneumatically operated. This piece of equipment makes very little noise and is dust-free. For those framers dealing only in wood moulding, and in a noise restricted area, this might be the cutting device to use.

There are two drawbacks, one is the fact that it will not cut metal moulding and secondly, angles other than 45°, such as for hexagons and octagons, are difficult to achieve.

Regardless of the machine or tool used to cut moulding, two things never vary, one is the allowance of 1/8" for ease of fitting (¼" for stretched oil paintings) and the other is the cutting of the long piece first.

Joining the Frame

Joining may be done either in the traditional hammer and nails method or by using semi-automatic joining systems. Whichever method is preferred, carpenters' glue must still be used. Many white glues dry brittle and are not waterproof. Hot melt glues are fast setting but are too thick for small corners. The glue should not be visible in the finished corners.

If nails or brads are used you will still need glue to hold the frame together. Excess glue should be wiped off immediately because it tarnishes some finishes. Nailing the corners requires planning. Make nail holes neat and evenly spaced. Before nailing, especially in hardwood, drill pilot holes to prevent splitting the moulding. Drilling can be done with a regular wood bit. The nails are countersunk and the holes filled.

There are several patterns of nailing (see examples below).

One method is nailing the top and bottom so nail holes will be less visible – **Figure A.**

Another method is from the sides to add strength especially for large frames – **Figure B.**

Cross nailing method adds strength but makes the frame difficult to separate should the need arise – **Figure C.** The 'rotation' method is another alternative – **Figure D.**

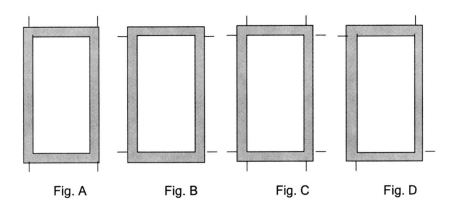

Fig. A   Fig. B   Fig. C   Fig. D

There are several other methods of joining corners using hand tools and pneumatic staplers and nail guns. A very efficient addition to the picture framing industry for joining picture frames is the under-pinner or V-nailer. This equipment, manually or pneumatically operated, forces a sharpened V-shaped wedge into the underside corner of the frame. It is strong, fast, neat, easy to apply and not visible. V-nails come in a variety of lengths and may be stacked for extra deep mouldings. Another simple, easy-to-use piece of equipment utilizes a router bit to cut out channels in the corners of the frame pieces. The corners are then glued and reinforced with plastic plugs inserted in the channels. The channels and plugs vary in length to accommodate shallow and deep mouldings.

Before the frames are put together it is a good idea to colour the edges of the moulding pieces with a marker pen of the same colour as the moulding finish. This prevents the light colour of the cut edge from showing.

Metal Mouldings

Of the materials available for making picture frames, aluminum is regularly selected for a wide variety of framing projects; the reasons for this being so are the adaptability, colours, look or style and the price. Although attempts in days past have been made to manufacture metal picture frame mouldings from tin, brass, iron and silver; aluminum metal has proven to be, by far, the most labour and cost effective.

The colours of metal moulding available vary from bright and radiant colours to a muted and frosted finish. The most popular finishes in metal mouldings are silver, gold and black.

Aluminum picture frame mouldings are manufactured by extrusion; that is, the metal is forced through a die by pressure. This process takes an aluminum ingot or billet, heated to about 870°F (465°C), placed into the extrusion press and forced through a designed form (die) to the required shape of the picture frame moulding. The lengths of moulding are then cut to standard sections, usually 10 or 12 feet in length. Once they are cooled, the mouldings are then "finished" in one of two methods—anodising or painting.

The anodising process requires many steps before completion. What it consists of are a series of cleaning processes and baths of various chemicals, depending on the desired finish. Electric current passes through the aluminum moulding and the chemical solution deposits the "colour" or finish on to the metal.

For painted moulding, once the aluminum has cooled from the extrusion process, high voltage is applied to the moulding which atomises the paint (the voltage does this) as it comes out of the paint spray nozzle. So, the paint is applied to the moulding by an electrostatic process. The painted moulding is then baked for 20 minutes at a temperature around 300°F (148°C).

Some of the popular metal profiles available are:

Advantages of metal mouldings over wood are:
- They are faster and less labour-intensive to cut and join.
- There is very little waste.
- Metal moulding does not warp or twist and there are no inherent imperfections such as knot-holes.
- It is easy to cut and store.
- It is durable and bound to endure.
- The price is generally lower.
- It has a nice clean, crisp look.
- It is chemically inert; there is no fear of acid or lignin content.
- The scraps are readily recycled.

Disadvantages in using metal rather than wood moulding:
- It is difficult to touch up a scratch on a metal frame.
- The framer cutting metal moulding must be aware of the danger possibility that pieces of moulding may fly off the saw blade if the saw is not enclosed.
- There are framing projects where no alternative to wood is required.

Quality aluminum moulding is very much in demand and is economical. New painted colours, metallic finishes, profiles and design concepts in using metal moulding have continued to keep up the excitement about aluminum.

Cutting Metal Mouldings

Metal mouldings are cut with electric powered saws. The type of saw blade used is usually 10" in diameter and varies from an 80- to 100-tooth carbide tipped blade to a 250-tooth blade similar to a plywood cutting blade but with no set. This latter blade almost totally prevents cut off pieces from being thrown, but it does need frequent sharpening. Whichever saw is used, the moulding must be clamped securely prior to cutting. In any case, it is imperative to use safety goggles and ear protectors.

Joining Metal Moulding

Metal frames are put together with hardware. There are two types of metal frames. One, called a back-loader, is joined at the corners with a strip of flat metal crimped with a special tool. The frame is completed and the contents are then put into the back and held in with metal springs or clamps. Clip hangers are inserted at the back of the frame.

The other, and by far the most common, uses two right-angled plates in each corner. One of the metal plates is tapped and has two screws while the other piece is blank. They are placed in the corners and the screws are then tightened. This type of frame requires three sides to be joined then the contents are slipped into place after which the fourth side is added. Springs are used to keep the contents to the front of the frame. The hangers used are either snap hangers or screw-secured types. Both require wire for hanging. For small pictures you may use a saw tooth hanger placed in the centre of the top frame section.

Polystyrene (Plastic) Mouldings

Although the word "plastic" is never used when discussing picture frames with customers, since in some people's minds it presumes an inferior product, this moulding meets the market demand of a segment of the picture framing trade and is an economically feasible framing option to other framing materials available. What the moulding is made of should not be an issue at the sales counter. What might be more important are its appearance, durability and price.

Similar to the manufacture of metal moulding, polystyrene (plastic) mouldings are extruded. Although some recycled plastics are used, the majority of moulding is manufactured from new material. Some characteristics about these mouldings worth noting are:

- They have very few defects—no warping, twisting or blemishes such as knots and splinters.

- They are sturdy, tough — not easily scratched or bruised and is easy to pack.

- The mouldings have a smooth surface so do not need burnishing

- They are good quality products finished in gilded, painted, embossed or varnished processes which can be made to look like wood moulding.

- The cost is considerably less than wood moulding; about one third the price.

- Large frames require reinforcing to prevent bending of the frame components.

- The cell structure of polystyrene is such that glues are not assimilated therefore special adhesives are necessary.

- Specific cutting and joining procedures are necessary; chopper blades must be very sharp requiring multiple small "bites" to avoid compressing the moulding; if a saw is used, it is advisable to use a high speed coarse-toothed blade, withdrawing the blade immediately after the cut to prevent melted plastic due to heat, from building up.

- It is advisable to do the cutting and joining in a well-ventilated area.

- New developments permit the use of (V-nailers) and nails for joining.

- Environmentally, consider that wood makes up about 7% of landfill space, and is bio-degradable, most plastics, on the other hand account for from 25% to 30% of garbage volume and are not bio-degradable.

Other Mouldings

Mica – this type of picture frame moulding consists of a mica laminate wrapped around a wood core. The core itself is kiln dried wood. The resulting product is straight, sturdy, and in effect, resists warping. Other advantages of mica mouldings are that they can look like wood with all its finishes and the almost infinite assortment of colours that are available. The cutting and joining is similar to that of wood.

Vinyl – vinyl wrapped mouldings are made of wood, usually pine, covered with thin plastic. The covering simulates wood grain, but it also comes in solid colours. It is inexpensive and yet has a quality appearance. Its price is attractive and a further value of vinyl wrapped moulding is its consistent uniformity of colour between sticks.

Liners

Liner

As the mat board is to paper art so the liner is to oil and acrylic paintings. Mat boards and liners serve similar purposes—to protect the artwork and make it look good.

Liners are often used for pictures that require visual separation from the frame. Although they are used principally when framing oils and acrylics, needle art is also framed using liners, especially if they are framed without glass. Liners are often described as "frames within frames" and provide a soft transition from the artwork to the frame and its environment.

The technique for framing with a liner is essentially the same as that used for the mitred frame. The liner should be close-fitted to the outer frame. Liners are often covered with fabric such as velveteen, linen, cotton, silk or synthetics. If the colour or fabric which you have in mind is not available in the commercial liner, it is quite easy to make your own liner using as its base a simple flat or round moulding and gluing the fabric into place. This, in fact, is a very satisfying and profitable part of picture framing. The adhesives available make it remarkably easy to do.

Fillets

A fillet is frequently the precise final enhancing detail to a framing job. Although fillets are used in close conjunction with frames, the greatest complementary placement is around the window opening of the mat next to the art. Fillets produce those additional lines of colour or dimension surrounding the art.

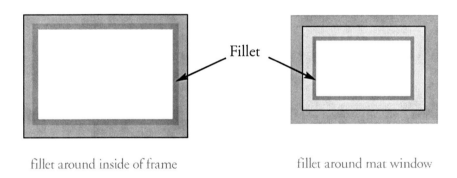

fillet around inside of frame   fillet around mat window

Although fillets are generally made of wood, there are plastic and metal fillets available but in every case it is the finish and the subtle proportions that make them attractive. The typical fillet has been gold-leafed but other finishes are on the market, finishes to match the frame or colours to emphasize some feature in the painting, similar to the function a second mat serves in paper art framing. Their use is varied and artistic, since they are an accent rather than an integral part of the frame. Fillets add prestige and value to the framing project on which they are used. In preparation for incorporating a fillet in the frame design:

- cut the window opening with a reverse bevel or a straight-cut opening.
- cut each side, or piece, of the fillet a bit longer than the mat opening in which it will be placed.

- trim the pieces until each one fits exactly; fillets are cut with a standard foot operated chopper or a portable chopper designed for this purpose.
- once the pieces are cut and trimmed to the right sizes, place them in their proper order and put a bit of tape on the underside to hold them in place.
- place the fillet frame on the table face up.
- apply ATG tape or other appropriate adhesive on the underside of the mat window opening and stick the fillet to it, press it into place.
- build up the back of the mat to the same level as the fillet using 100% acid free mat strips or acid free foam board; then apply acid free tape to the fillet and its adjacent filler board to ensure that the wood of the fillet is isolated from the art.

Specialty Frames—ovals, circles, octagons and others

Gift Ware and Craft Items

What to get for Aunt Jessie's birthday? The prospective customer looks with concern at the prices for art hanging on your walls. Even unframed art such as would please her aunt start at $45. Her budget will permit spending $40.

Is there anything else you could offer that might save this sale? Framing gallery/shop owners who have complementary items such as pottery, crafted jewellery and stained glass articles say that these objects draw in customers who normally would not find anything they liked or could afford. These same customers become repeat customers and in time purchased more expensive art.

Impulse Buyers – The main advantage of small gift items is that they draw in 'lookers' and gift-seeking customers. These articles build traffic and attract impulse buyers. They are especially well-suited to frame shops since impulse buyers are frequently those people who can afford custom framing.

But crafts and items other than framed art bring in people who are resolute about limiting their spending to under $50. But once they are in the framing gallery, they often see other things they like and end up buying more than one thing. Also, now and then, people who come with the objective of buying art or having custom framing done, spot a craft article they like and end up with another purchase. Studies on the habits of retail customers find that if something is under $50, people do not mind putting it on credit cards. So, if the items are priced between $15 and $30, and the person wants it, the person will get it.

There are also high-ticket items for the discriminating customer who is looking for a quality piece of pottery or an elegant sample of blown glass. It is to the gallery operator's advantage to be able to discuss with the customer how the item was made and where in the house it might be placed for full enjoyment.

Because small gifts and collectibles are, for the most part, directed at impulse buyers, proper marketing is imperative. A creative display is one way of showing off the various craft items, but another is to have them dispersed throughout the gallery. Craft pieces may be used to form part of the gallery's décor, however, the items must be price-tagged so the customers know they are for sale. A window display, changed periodically has definite drawing power.

Diversified Art – Craft and gift items should not be considered as second rate art, reserved solely for those who do not appreciate 'good' art. If the gallery owner discriminates in the types of craft items that are displayed, the gallery will soon establish a reputation for having a range of quality products. The gallery location will often dictate the types of items you should carry. Be sure to buy quality items that are equal to the quality of art you regularly carry.

CHAPTER SIX

V-Groove

A V-groove is an elegant line cut in a mat to disperse space, add design, and used as an outline for the main object. V-grooves can, however, be incorporated into various designs on the mat to highlight certain items in a collage, create a lattice effect and other patterns in rectangular, oval and circle openings of the mat. This type of cut exposes the core of the mat board using it as a factor of design. Once the skills of cutting a double mat have been attained, perhaps the next step is to learn how to do a V-groove.

Most mat cutters have a V-groove scale, stops, or peg settings to produce wide or narrow grooves. Get the mat cutter book out and practice cutting various widths and patterns of V-grooves.

Procedure:

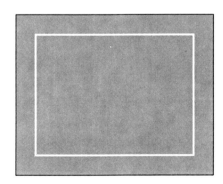

Mat Blank with V-groove

Mat with V-groove and opening

Method A.

1. Select a mat board 11" X 14".

2. Cut a "window" opening 2" from the edges.

3. Set the mat cutter for 1/16" or 3/32", depending on the width of the V-groove (again, refer to the mat cutter manual for this setting procedure).

4. Place the fallout under the cutter bar FACE UP and trim off the original bevel.

5. Replace and tape the fallout into the mat and cut a 2½" border.

Method B

1. Select a mat board 11" x 14".

2. On both the top and bottom of the mat board mark a 2" border with a pencil.

3. From the top side cut on the line but only ¾ of the way through.

4. From the bottom cut three sides all the way through and tape them up.

5. Cut the fourth side and tape it up.

6. With a sharp blade clean out the V-groove, if necessary; cut the 2½" border.

Inlay Mat

The design of an inlay mat is essentially a technique of placing pieces of mat board side by side to accommodate two or more colours in a mat and yet retain only one thickness of mat board. What this does is achieve one or all of the following objectives:

- Provides a look of *depth* for the print being matted without multi-layers of mat board.

- Decreases the thickness of the project for shallow moulding rabbets.

- Permits the use of non-glare glass without conspicuous image distortion.

There are several ways to cut and assemble an inlay mat, but here are a few suggestions that should be considered:

- When cutting, keep the same number of mat boards under the cutter bar.
- Use the same type (composition) of mat board for each part of the mat.
- Adjust the mat cutter blade to cut through one mat board thickness only.
- Practice.

1. Select a mat board 11" X 14"; this will be the outer or "top" mat.

2. Select a second piece for your "inlay" colour and cut it smaller than the "top" mat; similar to the double mat procedure.

3. Place the 'top' mat face side down on a table and stick the smaller mat (face down) to back of the "top" mat, using short pieces of double sided tape, near the outer edges.

4. Set the mat cutter guide to the 2½" border widths; remove the slip sheet.

5. Place the mat combination under the cutter bar—**face down** and cut the border. This is the window opening for the print.

6. Next, set the mat cutter guide to 2".

7. Cut from top to bottom on all four sides. Save the inlay and remove the remaining bits of mat board.

8. Replace the slip sheet but <u>do not disturb the mat guide setting.</u> Place the "top" mat under the cutter bar—**face down,** and cut the same border as in Step 6. Discard the fallout.

9. Place the inlay from Step 7 into the mat opening and tape the reverse side with 810 tape.

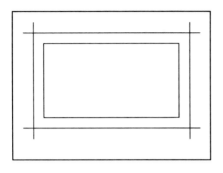

Reverse side   Inlay in place

To make a double inlay mat you would start off with three mats, of the selected colours, joined together similar to the single inlay procedure. Cut the window opening in the last mat board but with subsequent cuts make sure that you always have three layers of mat board under the cutter bar. The figure below illustrates the outcome of a double inlay mat.

J. Edwin Warkentin

Keystone Corner

The keystone corner design uses standard mat opening procedures and although it is more complex and may require patience and practice, the results are startling. Keystone mats have a remarkably systematic appearance. As with most artistic mats the keystone corner takes practice to achieve. Since this design takes longer than many other mat projects, remember to charge extra for them.

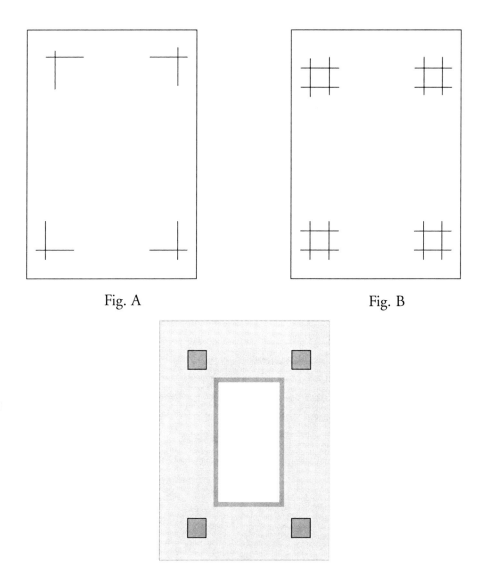

Fig. A   Fig. B

Fig. C

1. Select a mat board 11" X 14"; set the mat cutter guide bar at 1¾"; mark the back of the mat board as in Fig. A.

2. Move the guide bar to 2¼", mark the mat board, finishing up with ½" squares as shown in Fig. B. From the back, cut the four squares, make sure that the fallout is under the cutter bar at all times, so that the cut bevel is visible.

4. Now move the guide bar to 3", measure, mark and cut the window opening.

5. Finish the project by attaching a second mat which will be visible not only at the window opening but also in the square openings as in Fig. C.

6. Cut a 3¼" border.

Note:

1. Coloured paper may also be placed behind the square openings if a second mat is not required.

2. An alternative to the square openings might be to take the little square fallouts and V-groove' them, then tape them back into their respective openings. If this option is chosen be sure to number the squares and their location before cutting them out.

Arch And Cathederal Mat

Arch and cathedral mats incorporate circles and ovals with straight lines. The difference between the two arrangements is that the arch opening joins a circular or oval cut with straight sides while the cathedral opening adds a shoulder step or offset at the points where the rounded opening meets the straight lines. The latter is perhaps more artistic and it is certainly easier to achieve than the arch mat.

Both of these mat openings have pleasing applications for needlework, old photographs, portraits, and in some instances, object framing.

Arch Mat

By incorporating an arch design in your mat cutting repertoire your customers will be favourably impressed and you will enjoy the challenge. Your creativity along with the equipment at hand permit you to attempt the change from the ordinary.

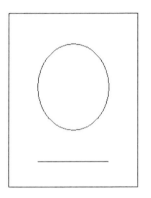 

Procedure:

1. Select a mat 11" X 14".

2. Measure and mark 2¾" side and bottom borders.

3. Measure 5½" from the side and 5¼" from the top for the centre of the circle.

4. Cut the 5½" circle (from the top side of the mat).

5. Cut the straight lines taking care to connect the sides so no obvious indication is apparent where they join the circle; this may be aided with an emery board.

Cathedral Mat (with offset)

The cathedral mat is another means of enhancing the framing project. Again, it can prove a very satisfactory method of framing old photographs, portraits such as wedding pictures, and needlework. One attractive feature of this type of opening is the small offset on either side of the circle. This is not only elegant in appearance but it provides an easy transition from the circle to the straight lines of the border without worrying about connecting points.

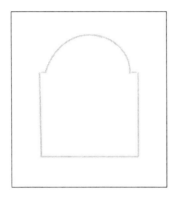

Procedure:

1. Select a mat board 11" X 14". With its centre 5¼" from the top of the mat board and 5½" from the each side, cut a 5½" circle. It is not necessary to cut the circle completely. The top of the circle will be 2½" from the top of the mat.

2. Cut the offsets 4¾" from the top — 3/16" each.

3. Cut the borders at 2 9/16" on sides and bottom.

4. To get around the large blank corners at the top, you might consider cutting a V-groove all the way around, 2" from the edge of the mat.

Long and Narrow

This configuration has an appeal for pictures or needle art that are physically long and narrow. By emphasizing these features with a mat weighted at both ends and making the side borders rather narrow the art's proportions are accentuated. The design of the mat opening is similar to the cathedral layout only in that you have the same type of construction at both ends of the opening. This arrangement lends itself especially to vertical art but there is no reason why horizontal projects should not be considered.

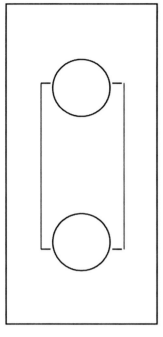

Fig. A

Fig. B

Procedure:

1. Select a mat board 6" X 14".

2. With centres at 35/16" from the ends of the mat board and 3" from the sides cut two 25/8" diameter circles.

3. Mark the offsets 3/16" at the edge of the circle lined up with the circle centres, or, in other words, 35/16" from the ends of the mat.

4. Draw the borders connecting the offsets as in Fig. A.

5. Cut the straight lines to complete the project as in Fig. B.

6. You might also consider cutting a V-groove one inch from the edges of the mat.

Kobe Corner

The decorative Kobe corner, although it has a unique oriental style, fits well to many other types of artwork including needlework. There are several forms of this cut. Some of them combine two overlapping circle cuts in each of the four corners with straight cuts for the mat border.

The method covered in this exercise is to utilize the "cathedral-cut-with-offset". In this technique there is no problem at the transition points of the arc and the straight line. It is artistic and adaptable to several art forms and relatively easy to achieve.

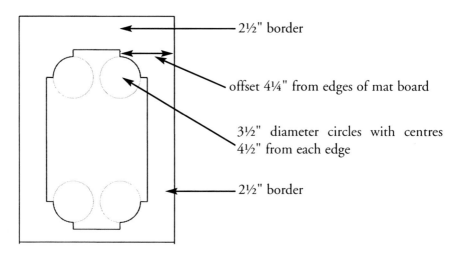

2½" border

offset 4¼" from edges of mat board

3½" diameter circles with centres 4½" from each edge

2½" border

Procedure:

1. Select a mat board 11" X 14".

2. Cut four 3½" circles centred at 4½" from both edges at each corner; replace the fallouts temporarily.

3. Measure and mark the borders and offsets.

4. Cut the offsets.

5. Cut the border.

Offset Corner

Offset corners lend a touch of design to what otherwise might be a plain window opening mat. Adding a V-groove strengthens the pattern even further.

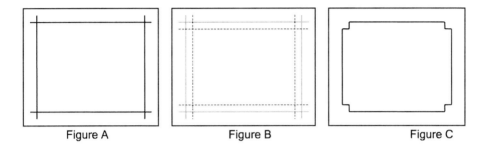

| Figure A | Figure B | Figure C |

Procedure:

1. Assume a mat border of 2¾"; measure and mark this border - Fig. A.

2. Move the cutter guide to 3" and mark the mat as shown by the dotted line in Fig. B.

3. While at the setting in Step 2, cut the dotted line from solid line to solid line on all four sides.

4. Return the cutter guide to 2¾" and cut the border but this time from dotted line to dotted line.

5. Fig. C is the finished product.

Contemporary Mat Design

This design is a variation on what has been known as the *contemporary* or *modern* mat arrangement.

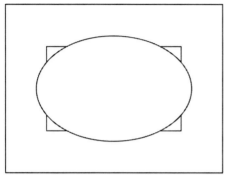 

Procedure:

1. On a mat board 11"X 14" draw a 2¼" border.

2. Cut an oval 8"X 11", from the front.

3. Tape the fallout back in, from the back.

4. Cut the 2¼" border.

5. Remove the tape and bits of mat board.

Double Bevel Mat

The heading title of this project might sound bewildering but what is required are two mat boards, the bottom cut to the image size and the top cut for a wide V-groove presentation with the two pieces attached to the bottom mat to give the arrangement a three-dimensional look. This aspect of the design might be further enhanced by placing foam board strips under the outside piece, lifting it up off the bottom mat.

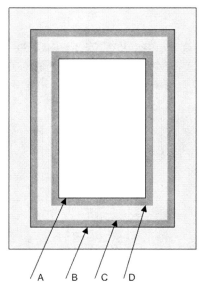

A   B   C   D

Procedure:

1. Select two mat boards 11"X 14". Cut a 2½" border on the bottom mat and put it to one side – Fig. A.

2. Cut a 2¼" border on the top mat – Fig. B

3. Now take the top mat and place it FACE UP under the cutter bar and cut a 1¾" border; save the fallout piece – Fig. C.

4. Cut a final border 1½", this time FACE DOWN – Fig. D.

5. Attach pieces Fig. B and Fig. C to the bottom mat.

French Matting

The artistry of French matting is coming into its own once again. During the 17th and 18th centuries in Europe, water-colour painting thrived. The mats available, which were neutral in colour, were then embellished with wash lines.

The border lines and muted washes, in between which tints of the water-colour were placed, became a form of enhancement. Mats so decorated, became known as "French mats". Artists frequently did the decorating themselves.

Originally, French mats were simply water-coloured panels bordered by contrasting accent lines on the face of the mat board. Today, French lines are smoother and easier to apply because of the availability of new materials and innovative techniques.

Common methods for designing and applying French lines use one or more of the following methods:

- pen lines of paint or ink
- coloured powder
- charting and pin stripe tape.
- water-colour paint
- "marbelized" paper

Decorative mats with French lines of various widths can be delicate and inconspicuous, thereby enhancing the artwork. French matting skills can be learned and developed. The surface of the mat board is important. For French matting the board, generally, is of museum or conservation quality, light in colour and smooth surface. These features permit the characteristics of water-colours to dominate. The colours and medium chosen, whether it is paint or ink, should be tested on a piece of mat board similar to the mat itself.

To identify and position the lines or panels, a mat marker guide (available from your supplier) is used to assure accuracy. Apart from the standard artists' paint brushes, the <u>ruling pen</u> is one of the most useful instruments in drawing French lines. One of its important features is that the width of the line may be varied with a slight adjustment. The pen must be kept clean when not in use, and although a firm, steady hand is required, pressure is not desirable when drawing the line. The way to success is <u>practice</u>.

The necessary equipment include:

- metal straight edge with cork or rubber back
- X-acto-type knife   pastel powders
- 811 removable tape
- white vinyl eraser
- mixing cup
- ponge brush.

Summary:

1. The pen must be kept clean at all times. Clean it immediately after use. Before putting the pen away, open the nib slightly to relieve pressure.

2. Let the medium flow smoothly. It is not necessary to apply pressure. Begin and complete a line in one unbroken motion.

3. Test the consistency (if using water colour) of the paint. Too thick paint will 'bead', too thin paint will 'bleed'.

4. Pens with curved blades should be held at a slight angle, in the direction of pen movement to let the ink or paint flow smoothly.

5. If the pen cannot hold enough paint or ink to finish a long line, let the first part of the line dry and then start the second portion where you left off. Do not go over a line once it is drawn.

6. To connect corners, the connecting line must be dry. The best method is to butt the lines up to each other.

7. The nib of the pen can be filled with an eye dropper or an artists' paint brush. Excess liquid should be removed to avoid unwanted paint migration.

8. Test the pen action and line width on a piece of mat board similar to the project to be undertaken. A fibre tipped pen is a good alter native to the ruling pen.

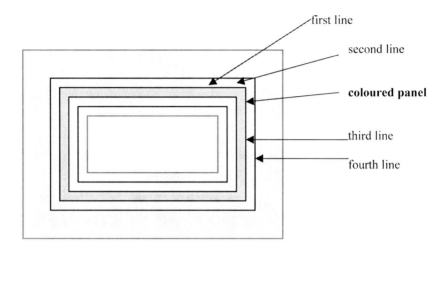

first line
second line
coloured panel
third line
fourth line

Ruling Pen

Water-colour Panel French Matting

This method uses water-colour paints in combination with several inked lines.

1. Select a mat board 11" X 14", measure, mark and cut a 3½" border.

2. Spray the board with a fixative—Blair Workable Spray Fixative, for example.

3. Lightly mark the location of two lines at the corners of the window opening.

4. Line up straight edge with the marks.

5. Fill the ruling pen with ink.

6. Starting with the line closest to the window opening, draw each one with one continuous stroke. Draw all the lines on one side, then the other side. Let these lines dry, then finish the other two sides and let them dry. These lines will act as a levee or "embankment" to

contain the paint.

7. Mix watercolour with water, in the mixing cup; test the colour for accuracy.

8. Using clear water, wet the panel space to ensure water-colour transfer.

9. A round, watercolour artists' paint brush is used. A small amount of sugar may be added to the water to slow down the drying; the same may be done to the watercolour paint.

10. Start applying the watercolour paint (again, with the artists' brush) away from the corner and pull it around the panel. It helps if you tilt the mat board down in the direction you want the paint to flow. Keep the panel wet.

Limited Edition Prints

They are just that—prints. However, they are high quality reproductions from original artwork. The number is strictly limited (the original plates and film are destroyed once the quality and printing are approved). Each print is signed by the artist and consecutively numbered, giving each one an individual identity.

These prints are generally multicoloured replicas of an image on fine, acid-free art stock. The signature which the artist places on each print verifies that the artist has examined and approved the print.

Verification signatures are done in pencil. The signature verifying authenticity and quality are done in pencil, a practice that began in the mid-19th century. Pencils were used because of the limitations of other media available at the time. Pencils, unlike ink pens, were part of the artist's sketch box. It was distinctive from the artwork yet did not detract from the artwork. If left alone, pencil lines are permanent. They will not discolour, bleed or act on the paper fibres.

Pencil lead is a combination of graphite and clay. The pressure of the drawing stroke not only forces these particles into the fibres of the paper but also creates a slight gloss by causing the particles to take a flat-level position.

How large should the edition be? The term "limited edition" implies out of the common run or hard to find. As with other commodities of limited number, owning one becomes a point of prestige and self-esteem. Owning a limited edition print engenders a measure of satisfaction in possessing a piece of art that is obtainable only in restricted numbers.

Many connoisseurs of fine art find fault with those publishers who print large editions, maintaining that such practices compromise the market for limited edition prints and diminish buyer confidence in the value of such artwork. One critic contends that customers shy away from large edition prints, looking upon them as almost an open edition. Others believe that a large edition is equivalent to poor quality. The size of the edition does not in itself have anything to do with quality.

So then, what size edition? Those in the art selling business have definite views on what size limited editions should be. The problem is that very seldom do two experts agree on the ideal number. Where they do agree is that edition sizes and prices could be adjusted to provide greater earnings for both the artist and the publisher.

The secondary market of small editions, which frequently sell out quickly, has at times resulted in a rapid price increase bringing a sizeable return to the owner, giving a perception of fast profits. Operators of galleries who deal in secondary market art to their customers have a responsibility to inform them regarding the risks of investing in art for quick financial returns rather than for art enjoyment. Their art might eventually increase financially but there is no guarantee of it.

CHAPTER SEVEN

Education

Preparation for Picture Framing

What, go to school to learn picture framing?

Are the advantages worth the time and expense?

Specifically, what is there that might benefit me?

Picture framing schools are equipped to put custom framers on the vanguard of framing techniques and understanding business. However, a large problem that affects many trades requiring broad skills and knowledge is to convince picture framers to upgrade their competence by attending framing classes to acquire new skills as well as keep up to date with changes in equipment and techniques in the business. Proficiency is not necessarily equated with years of experience. Craftsmanship is the measure of competence. The more informed and current framers are, the more likely they will stay in business.

Schools in different countries or even regions in the same country use various approaches for teaching picture framing. Each procedure is not necessarily superior or inferior to the others; a lot depends on each student's needs or choices.

The benefits of taking formal training exceed by far the duration and the cost. The demand for high quality workmanship has increased partly because customers have become more knowledgeable regarding techniques and materials that should be used to preserve their art. Competent framers must learn and adapt current methods in order to remain dependable. Where once the three basic criteria for framing were cheap, cheap and cheap, today's customers demand service, quality, and value. People visiting show homes, art galleries or even commercial establishments such as hotels displaying art admire the quality of the displayed pictures and want what they see for their own homes. So, when they go to see their local picture framer to have their artwork framed they are quite likely to ask for double mats, inlays, coloured core mats, French lines, conservation glass and etched glass. The professional framer must know how to deal with these requests.

What is there that might benefit me?

The demand for differently applied techniques and decorative additions has increased in recent years. This has been brought about, partly, because some innovative and perhaps adventurous framer has displayed what could be done. Twenty years ago retailers could get by with presenting little diversity in their products and services. Picture framers were among these groups. Framers who are unable to provide current techniques will, before long, lag farther and farther behind. Training often helps reduce time and money wasted learning from mistakes. Courses taught at most framing schools will show you the correct way.

The Centre de Formation Paris a school in France that is considered high level, runs a professional five year full time course for framers. Some framers with an inactive or negative approach to training consider five years as being a colossal waste of time with comments like, "Five years! What could you possibly do for five years?"

A noted picture framing consultant states that a work of art should be able to be returned to its original state at any time. These skills need to be learned. Even though most countries, France excepted, do not have picture framing laws; framers should be able to perform their work properly and professionally. This applies in particular to conservation/preservation framing. A framer should at least know how to take care of a piece of work entrusted to him/her.

Almost all picture framing schools provide basic framing courses for the novice. Some offer specialized or advanced courses including object

(3D) framing, French matting, image transfer, creative matting, needlework framing, glass etching, glass mats, gilding and restoration techniques. Most schools offer business management courses as part of the regular curriculum.

Who attends these schools?

Most of the students attending classes are inexperienced. Some are hobby framers and artists, many of whom, as a survey showed, soon gravitate to become full time framers. Long-time picture framers, generally speaking, do not attend formal courses. They often have a defensive mind-set towards education of this type. Their rationale ranges from time pressures to the opinionated view that there would be little to be gained from training due to their extensive experience in the business.

Upon interviewing many students in basic and advanced courses who had finished the typical five-day programs offered by most framing schools, the comments, almost without exception, were that the courses were not long enough since there was so much to learn. The majority of students who had taken the basic training returned for more specialized courses if they were offered.

School Profiles

There is an assortment of organizations that conduct picture framing courses. These include the private framer who has amassed many years of experience and is now passing it on to other framers or would-be framers. Usually this type of person represents an independent school. They maintain that, through experience, they are better able to present unbiased guidance on supplies and equipment.

Then there are the suppliers and distributors of framing materials and equipment. Their claim is that they sell the best equipment and materials available to help the framer do the best work possible in the least amount of time which then reflects positively in the profit margin. They suggest that they are in the best position to give advice since they regularly attend trade shows around the world and note the latest improvements and techniques in the picture framing industry. Several distributors stated that they had started out as framers; they recognized the potential problems facing picture framers and so could offer practical assistance.

And then there are the picture framing guilds and associations. The organizations tend to offer seminars and workshops that last from a few hours to a couple of days. These courses are focused with immediate applications to the industry. The venue is usually at a trade show or in suppliers' facilities.

The student/teacher ratio varies greatly from two to 20 per class. Of course the smaller the class the more individual attention is given to students. Most schools have a fixed curriculum. Changes are incorporated as new materials, equipment and methods become available. Although most advanced courses are scheduled along a similar fixed pattern, there is greater flexibility which allows students to pick and choose which topic will benefit them the most. Weekend classes have become important for framers who are unable to free up time in the week.

The structured classroom type of program presents certain advantages especially where students each have their own workspace and mat cutter. The exchange of ideas and aspirations among students is also beneficial.

Summary

When you have completed the program, you will:
- Have learned how to operate a frame shop competently and be a professional framer.
- Have used professional equipment and employed the latest techniques.
- Now operate the frame shop as a business including promotion and advertising techniques.
- Find your income has increased through efficiency.

Code of Ethics

1. Observe the highest principles of integrity in all dealings.

2. Defend and protect the interests of your customers.

3. Avoid the use of dishonest, baffling, incorrect or deceptive terms and descriptions.

4. Make every attempt to arrive at an agreeable and prompt solution in the event of a disagreement with a customer.

5. Provide sufficient insurance protection to be appropriate to your business and your customers' needs.

CHAPTER EIGHT

Conservation/Preservation

Introduction

- What is conservation/preservation framing?
- What feature(s) determines whether art requires conservation treatment?

Conservation framing is a common term understood by much of the general public for the way valuable, original watercolours, limited edition lithographs, drawings, etchings, or art of sentimental/historical importance ought to be framed. It is a term used by many picture framers to describe how those items will be treated. A better word might be _preservation_, since preservation rather than conservation of art is what is being attempted. As the number of serious art buyers is growing, and these buyers are becoming more aware of preservation framing, so custom picture framers had better become aware of preservation framing techniques and keep up with new materials and methods.

Preservation includes materials used that will protect the art. Preservation also implies, in fact demands, that the procedure is readily reversible; again, without altering the art in its original state.

The "amount" of preservation processes applied to a piece of art is really not a point for debate since, although there may be several levels of general framing, there is no such thing as 50% or 75% preservation framing. And the term _acid-free_ does not automatically mean the same thing as *conservation.* In conservation/preservation mounting and framing, although acid-free components and UV filtering glass are especially important, you must consider other aspects which are equally important, such as reversibility, potential physical damage to art, method of handling art and assembling or fitting the total package.

Art must be handled by the edges and then with clean hands or preferably with gloves. The paper on which the art is printed must not be folded or cut, since it could not then be restored to its original state.

Mounting Boards

Although some framers use acid-free corrugated cardboard and/or acid-free foam boards for mounting art in a preservation way, conservators reject these materials for that purpose. In the manufacturing of acid-free cardboard, chemicals are included which have the potential to give off harmful gases such as sulphur oxides. Acid-free foam board has the capacity to discharge gaseous polymer styrene, a solvent for plastic, which may cause concern where the art medium includes plastic. The covering papers of foam board might very well be acid-free, but it is the plastic between the covers that must be considered where art is concerned.

The material to which art should be hinged is 4-ply rag board or its equivalent in quality. For large pieces of art you might want to consider 6- or 8-ply mat board. The filler board (placed behind the mounting board to provide stability and strength) should be of equal quality. To assume that corrugated cardboard might be acceptable since it is located some distance from the art itself, at best compromises preservation framing and at worst invites possible disaster with its consequences.

Mat Boards

The pH scale, as discussed in a previous section, by which the suitability of many framing components including mat boards are measured, must be made clear. pH is a measure of acidity and alkalinity. The symbol "pH" is a measure of how much free acid is present in a moist environment. Paper, under normal conditions as far as humidity and temperature are concerned, contains close to 6% water.

Mat board manufacturers customarily provide the pH value of their boards in their technical specification sheets. Ideally, mat boards should record a pH of between 7.5 and 9.5 with an alkaline reserve of 1 to 3 *per cent* in order to meet preservation standards. What you want to look for is a pulp that does not include lignin. Cotton and purified bleached wood fall into this category. There are other components that go into the manufacturing of mat boards, such as: necessary binding ingredients used in sizing, adhesives and colour components. Highly acidic chemicals, such as alum, will jeopardize the acid-free raw materials. Aluminum Sulphate, $Al_2(SO_4)_3$, is used extensively in paper manufacturing. The sulphate radical, SO_4, when combined with water produces sulphuric acid, H_2SO_4. Pigments or dyes used in coloured boards are further factors to be considered, especially the binding agent for dyes. Pigments are more fade- and bleed-resistant than most dyes. Some dyes may include an acidic binding ingredient used to maintain the colour, although that does not apply to all dyes.

Cotton is the purest and most stable type of cellulose, consisting of 99% cotton cellulose and 1% lignin. Wood pulp contains about 20% to 30% lignin. Both types of pulp, cotton and wood, are thoroughly bleached to eliminate the lignin present. Bleached fibres are referred to as alpha cellulose, and the bleaching agent is calcium carbonate ($CaCO_3$). Lignin (a part of cellulose which itself is stable) is chemically unstable. Lignin, in fact, is extremely sensitive to light and heat. When stimulated by light or heat, it becomes very acidic and attacks cellulose. The presence of lignin causes paper to self-destruct. It is for this reason that mat boards made of ground wood or unbleached wood must not be used in preservation framing. This type of mat board is referred to as "regular" and is perfectly satisfactory to use with impermanent framing, such as posters, that do not require special preservation treatment.

Mounting

Whether or not the artwork is to be framed with or without a mat, it must be attached to a mounting or backing board. The mounting board must be of at least 4-ply rag board-quality board, although for small pieces of art 2-ply rag board is adequate. The problem with the lighter weight mounting board as it affects larger pieces of art is that it (the 2-ply) tends to buckle under the art's weight.

Attaching artwork to mounting boards is just as important. Since paper expands and contracts with humidity and temperature changes, the method used must ensure that the art's movement is not limited to the extent that it could become wrinkled. In other words, artwork must be held securely in place and yet be allowed to expand and contract as determined by its environment. There are several methods to solve the problem, but the only *real* procedure is to use hinges. Hinges for preservation mounting come under the general heading of Japanese tissue.

Japanese paper, actually a tissue, comes in different weights, strengths and even colours. It is important to find a good hinge with suitable strength to support the art but must also be weak enough to tear if necessary (should the framed picture fall off the wall) and so save the art. In the event that you select proper Japanese paper for the art item being mounted, hinges will be sufficiently strong. At all times use paper that is the same weight, or slightly less than the art item itself. When selecting Japanese paper for hinging, stipulate handmade, papers purged clear of regular wood pulp content. A preferred assortment of Japanese papers includes Kizukishi, Uda, mulberry, and Sekishu—mulberry, handmade rom sulphite and kozo pulp is favoured.

The long fibres in a sheet of Japanese paper run parallel to the chain lines which may be seen running across the paper approximately an inch or so apart, when held up to a light. This provides remarkable strength to the paper when applied in this direction.

Place a straight edge along about one inch from one end of the Japanese paper. Next, with either a ruling pen or fine paint brush, apply distilled water alongside the straight edge. The strip can now be pulled apart along the wetted line.

The artwork should be hung from the top by either pendant or V-type hinges, customarily near the top corners. Heavy or oversize artwork will in all probability require extra hinges. Do not overdo it, since paper artwork must be permitted to expand and contract with temperature and humidity changes. An unbroken strip of hinging, for example, prevents movement resulting in ripples being formed adjacent to the hinge. V-hinges, especially ones that have been reinforced with a cross tab, are preferred for cases where a mat is not a requirement or where the attractive deckle edges of the paper want to be visible. This also applies to papyrus art.

Pendant hinges

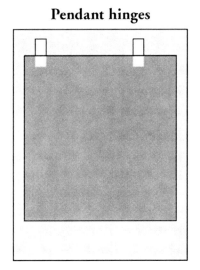

T-hinges

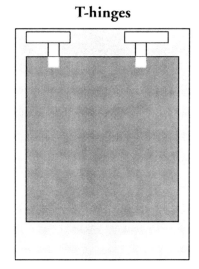

Another form of "hidden" hinges is the S-hinge. This type requires that slits be cut in the mount board with the hinges threaded through.

Hinge application and locations:

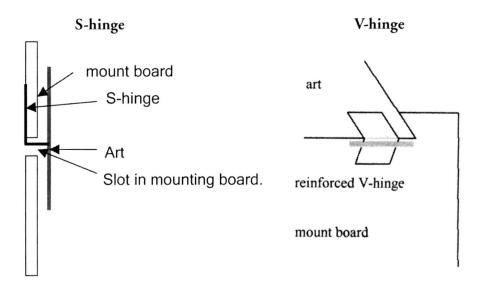

S-hinge

mount board

S-hinge

Art

Slot in mounting board.

V-hinge

art

reinforced V-hinge

mount board

Adhesives

Proper adhesives for conservation mounting are mandatory in preserving paper-borne works of art. Although one often looks for short cuts when conducting work, in the case of conservation framing, and especially where adhesives are concerned, there are no short cuts.

As tempting as using linen and pressure-sensitive tapes are, their very composition invalidates them as hinging materials. They are much stronger than the art they support, so if the framed item is jolted, the paper will tear before the tape lets go. The glue used in their adhesive is also very strong and not water-reversible. Adhesive used for these tapes cannot be totally dislodged. Linen tape, however, is conventionally used to hinge the mat to the mounting or backing board. In the case of a portrait-style (vertical) arrangement, the tape hinge is attached so the project opens like a book; if the layout is in the landscape (horizontal) format, tape is attached at the top.

So then which adhesive is used in conservation/preservation framing? For decades, we might say centuries, conservators have viewed that the best types of adhesive pastes were wheat starch and rice starch. (Follow instructions on the starch containers.)

Methyl cellulose adhesive has gained acceptance for conservation mounting, although it does not have the holding power of starch-based adhesives. There are several qualities about methyl cellulose worth considering. It does not have to be cooked, which is the case for both starch pastes. Just mix some of the powder with distilled water, let it sit a while until it forms a clear, gelatinous consistency, at which time it is ready for use. It does not discolour, resists mould and has a longer shelf life than do the starch-based adhesives

Whichever adhesive is chosen look for the following characteristics:

- 100% acid-free
- easily prepared
- water-based; readily reversible
- non-staining
- non-toxic
- resistant to fungus and insects.

Assembling the Hinges

Place the art face down on a clean sheet of paper or the reverse side of a mat board.

1. Place the hinges on a piece of blotting paper and with a small paint brush apply the paste sparingly to ¼" at the end of the hinge; in other words only this part of the hinge will be attached to the art work.

2. Let the hinges remain on the blotter until the paste has lost its glossy appearance. Very carefully apply the hinges to the art a small distance from the corners of the art. Place blotters over the hinges to pick up excess moisture.

3. Place a piece of glass over the blotters and add some weights on top of the glass. Let the adhesive set and dry—about 15 minutes.

4. Turn the artwork with hinges attached into its proper location on the mounting board with reference to the mat opening.

5. Place weights on the art to hold it in place while the hinges are attached to the mounting board. Apply adhesive to the under side of the hinges, place the blotting paper on the hinge and weights as in 4, above.

6. A cross tab of the same material as the hinges may be added using the same adhesive.

Mounting Alternatives

Many new accessories for mounting artwork have appeared in the past decade. Although by preservation standards the only appropriate materials are Japanese paper hinges and wheat starch or rice starch adhesives. There are factors that framers frequently face which cause them to consider alternatives. Among these are time pressures, demands of the customer, the worth or importance of the piece to be framed. There are safe alternatives but their composition, especially method for removal must be taken into account.

Self-adhesive Mylar corner pockets are available in various sizes (Fig. A. below). Corner pockets may also be handmade from 100%

cotton-based paper, from strips of Japanese paper. The bottom of the art will rest on the bottom corners but the sides and top corners will be positioned 1/16" away from the art itself. The corners are held in place by either starch paste or linen tape.

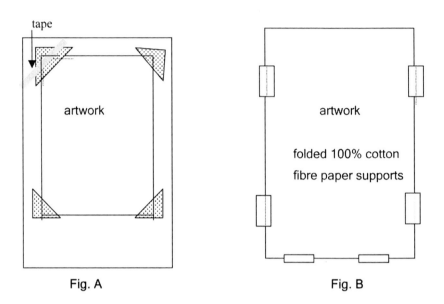

Fig. A   Fig. B

Mounting strips (Fig. B. above) are folded and placed at the bottom, sides and top of the artwork and attached to the mounting board with starch pastes. The art will rest on the bottom channels but the top and side mounting strips must be positioned 1/16" away from the art to permit movement during temperature and humidity changes.

Glazing Components

When light strikes a piece of glass or acrylic, some light is cast back, or reflected, some is absorbed while the rest is passed through. Unless the glazing material is treated in some way, ultraviolet (UV) rays will also pass through.

Ultraviolet radiation from the sun directly or indirectly, as well as light radiating from most fluorescent lamps, react with inks in the art causing chemical reactions which in turn fades colours. Shorter wavelengths of visible light radiating from ordinary incandescent light bulbs also cause damage especially to indigo and blue. The diagram below illustrates the location of ultraviolet rays in the frequency spectrum:

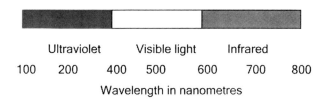

Ultraviolet   Visible light   Infrared

100   200   400 500   600   700   800

Wavelength in nanometres

Ultraviolet (UV) and infrared (IR) rays are considered luminous (radiant) energy. Filtering of UV can be attained by utilizing UV absorbing glazing materials. Fluorescent lighting tubes, for example, may be covered with plastic covers which absorb up to 98 per cent of UV present. Conservation glass provides artwork with maximum possible UV protection, around 98.9 per cent. Conservation glass is produced by a special UV-absorbing optical coating fused onto top of quality glass—the side which will be placed closest to the artwork. The coating is clear, but the glass itself comes in clear or with reflection controlled surfaces.

Another type of conservation glass has an optically coated plastic film sandwiched between two 1mm sheets of glass. This laminating film in both cases has the capacity of absorbing up to 99 per cent of ultraviolet radiation in the range of 100 to 400 nanometres.

An absorbent component is added to the formula during the manufacture of ultraviolet-filtering acrylic. This type of acrylic has the potential for the same filtering quality as its glass counterpart. It has the added advantage of being light weight and, within reason, shatterproof.

Cleaning of conservation glazing is rather important. Cleaners containing either acetic acid or ammonia or other unknown components as part of the formula should be cause for concern since there is a danger of their residues remaining on the glass. Water and a chamois or other lint-free drying cloths are preferred. If there are deposits on the glass that are resistant to water, try some isopropyl alcohol, finishing it off with water and lint-free chamois.

Frames

Of some importance is the frame for artwork so that no components of the moulding will degrade preservation activities. For all intents and purposes, metal frames are chemically inert, so nothing needs to be done to make them conservation-safe. What might be considered is sealing the back of the frame with linen tape to prevent pollutants and vermin from gaining access to the art.

The rabbet of a wood frame is sealed by applying two coats of polyurethane or a sealing tape such as Mylar or aluminum foil. This procedure prevents chemicals in the wood from out-gassing with possible harmful effects to artwork. A dust cover of 1-ply conservation board is glued or taped to the back of the frame, again, to prevent dust or other pollutants from encroaching on the art.

Encapsulation of Fragile Art

Encapsulation is a highly protective method of preserving important documents, antique items such as marriage certificates, land title deeds, newspaper clippings, sport cards and many other articles of personal interest.

A preparatory step to encapsulation is the de-acidification of the paper. Newsprint is especially troublesome because it is made of ground wood pulp which is naturally acidic, meaning that it will gradually "self-destruct." Although de-acidification will not remove the acid content in paper, it will neutralize it to prevent further deterioration. Paper degradation may be slowed by the application of commercial de-acidification products, available through conservation material distributors.

In encapsulation, the artwork is placed between two sheets of 3 - 5 mil. polyester film which is free of plasticizers and is pH neutral; Mylar is such a film.

- cut the film approximately one inch larger than the artwork on each side
- put the art on a hard, flat surface, lay one of the films on the art and with a weight on top to hold it in place, attach double-sided tape around the perimeter of the film; leave corners of the tape open to

allow air to escape— see illustration below.

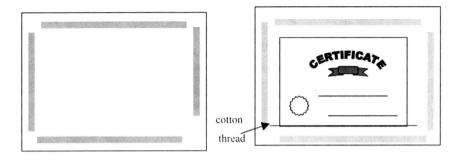

cotton
thread

- run a cotton thread just above the tape of the bottom side as a precaution against the art coming in contact with the tape if it should slip down.
- remove the weight and centre the art on top of this film, put the second film piece on top and place the weight on top to prevent the items from shifting
- lift one side of the top film and remove the backing paper from the double-sided tape; then repeat this on the other three sides.
- burnish the film to the tape.
- the film "sandwich" can be hinged to the mounting board and a mat is cut to conceal the taped edges.

Summary

- Sunlight is a greater threat to artwork than artificial light, as it contains stronger ultraviolet (UV) rays. Both direct and indirect sunlight cause damage. UV rays cause colours to fade and the lignin (tree sap) in wood-based paper to go brown. If wood-based paper has had the lignin removed and has been buffered to pH neutral with calcium carbonate (chalk) it should not go brown when exposed to UV rays. Some modern prints are printed with light-fast inks. Antique colours and dyes are particularly prone to fading.

- Changes in temperature and humidity are a threat to artwork on paper. Very dry conditions cause paper to dehydrate and thus become brittle and crack or flake; this problem is exacerbated in modern life with the regular use of central heating and air conditioning. Galleries and art collectors often have humidifiers to keep humidity constant. Damp conditions are often the home to fungus and mould; these tend to flourish at the back of pictures which are away from light (which kills mould spores) and where damp is retained the longest. Damp also tends to leave brown tidemarks as it dries. Paper expands as its fibres become waterlogged and contracts as these dry out; this process can cause paper to wave and ripple.

- Artwork must not be restricted from expanding and contracting, that is, it should not be taped to the mounting board on all four sides. This would probably result in cockling or rippling, but, with extreme changes in humidity, it may even tear. It should be hinged to the mounting board with T-shaped paper hinges, which are attached to the back of the artwork, overlapping onto it as little as possible.

- Conservation-quality paper corners can be used to attach artwork to the mounting board (these work on a similar principle to the corners used to stick photographs in albums). The advantage of this method is that no adhesive comes in contact with the artwork. Expansion and contraction can occur even more freely than if the artwork were attached with a couple of hinges, so cockling is less likely (care must be taken to ensure that the corners, when positioned, leave space for expansion—except at the bottom of the bottom corners on which the artwork rests). These paper corners come in a range of sizes or can be made easily by the framer. Paper corners cannot be used if there is insufficient border around the image or if the artwork is on very thin paper which may sag.

- Ideally, the paper hinges used to attach artwork are torn, not cut. This is because a cut edge can, over time, result in a harsh line appearing on the front of the artwork; a torn edge is softer and more gradual.

- Artwork should be attached to the mounting board, not to the back of the mat. This has become accepted practice in museums because the artwork is thus supported by a flat back and is less likely to be torn when the mat is opened up.

- The pH scale, reading from 0 to 14, is a measure of acidity and alkalinity. A reading of pH7 conveys that the material in question is neutral, that is, neither acid nor alkaline. Materials used in conservation framing must show a reading of pH7 or higher—more alkaline; if the reading is lower than pH7 the material has an unacceptable acid content. It is a good thing if materials have a higher pH than 7, as this allows for a little deterioration over time without the condition of the artwork being compromised.

- Boards used in conservation framing should be a minimum of 4-ply thickness for both the mat and the mounting board. A mat of this thickness allows sufficient distance between the glazing and the artwork in most cases, though pastels and other original work with loose pigments or thick paint may require a double mat. A thick mounting board provides a strong support. If a spacer is used instead of a mat, this too should be at least the thickness of a 4-ply mat board.

- Mat board used for conservation framing should be light-fast and bleed resistant. If the colour of the mat fades, the framed picture will look less attractive. The light-fastness of dyes and pigments is measured by a system developed by the Technical Association of Pulp and Paper Industries (TAPPI) and by the Blue Wool Scale (Britain). Two small pads or "bumpers" should be attached to the back of the frame at the bottom corners, to allow air circulation over the back of the picture and to prevent the frame from marking the wall. These bumpers look neat and impress customers.

- Many framers back frames with Kraft (brown or black wrapping paper) paper. This material is very acidic, which is why a thick, acid free mounting board is required. Framers have started using acid-free foam-centred boards as fillers in the back of the framed picture because the centres are chemically inert, the facing and backing papers are pH neutral, it is light in weight and rigid. Foam-centred board is more expensive than the traditional backing materials, such as corrugated cardboard, so tends to be used only for conservation work. Backing board should be a minimum of 4-ply thickness and 3/16" for large items. A sheet of aluminum or chemically inert plastic is sometimes inserted between the mounting board and the backing, or filler board; this offers added protection from the backing board and from impurities, insects and damp that may penetrate the picture from the back.

Art Auctions

Your gallery can sponsor recurring art auctions as an added attraction to bring in customers. An auction sale provides customers with an opportunity to sell art which they no longer want, or an opportunity to enhance their collected works.

People's preferences in art change from time to time. It is quite natural to grow weary of a certain piece. Auction sales give customers a chance to change their art.

Art auctions also give the gallery owner an opportunity to sell slow-moving art inventory. How many of us have had art on our gallery walls year after year with very little customer interest? So, for these auctions, art is assembled from customers' homes, from storage warehouses and from other dealers in art. It is the gallery staffs, who decide which pieces are to be offered for auction. If this is done professionally, the art offered will help draw people. You will find that the public will bring in all types of art and, although a variety is desirable, periodically you might want to concentrate on selected categories, such as wildlife; or to promote certain artists.

You want to retain auctioneers who are familiar with the types of items being sold. They are paid by commission, at a standard rate for each piece sold. All art is taken on consignment by the gallery. Registering the art requires a small fee from the customers. The gallery pays the owners of the sold artworks.

Customers should be cautioned to not expect a fortune from their art in this way. From the gallery's point of view, the sales kindle an interest in art and encourage old customers to participate and not to generate big profits. It is more of a public relations activity.

CHAPTER NINE

Mounting Methods

Which mounting technique and which adhesive to use for each framing project is a cause for concern among picture framers, especially newcomers to the trade. Customers bring in just about anything to be framed and everything must be mounted in one way or another. Items include fabric art, fine art, posters, photographs, three dimensional objects and artwork of various media. The key is in knowing what method and adhesive is best. Then, the next concerns are what products are available and how they should be used. The adhesive you decide on will be determined by the requirements of the artwork being mounted as well as the mounting process used.

Once the techniques and adhesives have been investigated, the choice comes down to what is best for the item to be mounted keeping in mind the responsibility of the professional picture framer.

The mounting process for flat art generally falls into two classifications: *cold* and *hot*. Both require adhesives and there is an extensive selection range of adhering substances. There is also the matter of selecting equipment to apply the adhesive. If no equipment is at hand, wet mounting is probably the only choice.

Wet Mounting

This is one of the oldest methods of attaching paper art onto mount boards. The water-based adhesive is thinned down until its density is compatible with the application method. Although there are several commercial pastes on the market, the best, from environmental and quality outlook is made from water-based reversible vegetable starch, such as wheat starch. The paste is applied with a brush or roller to either the artwork or the mount board. Pastes are also available in spray cans and others are applied with spray guns. The print usually comes rolled up, making the application of adhesive difficult. If that is the case, the paste should be applied to the mount board.

The mounting takes place in a clean, dust-free environment. The print is placed face down on a piece of paper on a clean surface. The back of the print is uniformly dampened with a sponge. This expands the print and makes it easier to handle. Place the mount board on the dampened print to keep it flat and moist. Apply the paste to the mount board. Make sure that no lumps or other foreign particles such as dust are in the paste. Turn the pasted mount board over and apply it to the back of the print. Then turn the whole project over including the paper on the face of the print but see that it does not shift thereby smearing paste onto the face of the print.

Hand rub the print with the paper still intact, commencing from the centre and working out to the edges. Check that no speck of dirt is under the print because dirt specks cause objectionable pits on the print. If something is under the print that should not be there, lift the print and remove the "thing."

While the paper is still damp and after the print is mounted, paste a sheet of paper, preferably the same weight paper as the print, to the reverse side of the mount board. This keeps the print flat while drying. As a further precaution, place the mounted print under some weights until the whole project is dry. If a vacuum press is available place the print in the activated press, under pressure, for several minutes.

To mount a large item such as a poster, map or blueprint using the "wet" method, mark the mount board exactly where the print has to go. Apply the paste to the mount board as in the previous method. Place a sheet of adhesive-resistant paper, such as release paper, on the pasted board, but just under the locating marks you made. Place the back-dampened print on the release paper adjusting the top up to the marks and gradually slide out the release paper, burnishing the print with your hand as the release paper is withdrawn.

Fabrics can be mounted with cloth paste but you must be careful to control the amount of adhesive that is applied to the mount board. Apply a thin coat of paste. To ensure that excess paste is removed, and thereby preventing it from saturating the fabric, put a sheet of Kraft (brown or black wrapping paper) paper right on the pasted board pressing it into the paste then remove it, leaving a skim of paste. This is especially important when dealing with sheer fabrics such as silk. Before placing the fabric on the paste, make sure that the weave is straight or the pattern is uniform. Again, it is advisable to counter-mount, that is, paste a sheet of heavy paper to the reverse side of the mount board to stop warping.

Vacuum Mounting

The vacuum press system uses adhesives and pressure provided by a press designed for that purpose. The vacuum press produces pressure by pumping out the air between the rubber membrane base and a lid thereby creating a powerful force. The artwork pasted to a mount board is squeezed between the membrane and the lid thereby creating an effective bond.

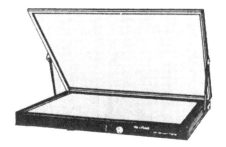

Vacuum Press

The adhesive may be sprayed from a pressurized can or applied with a brush or roller. Again, watch that no dust speck or other foreign matter gets into the paste.

Vacuum mounting is fast. It is also safer for items with a sensitive surface since no heat is involved. Once you have the press, this is perhaps the least expensive method of mounting. A disadvantage of course is that the size of the press limits the size of mounting you can do.

If mounting on foam board you should allow an extra inch on each side of the mount board to allow for the edges which will be crushed by the press. An alternative is to place pieces of foam board around the mount board to take the force of the pressure. Prior to applying the adhesive, you might want to roughen the mount board surface with fine sandpaper or steel wool to provide a superior bonding surface.

Pressure Sensitive

This is an alternative cold mounting procedure where no equipment is required and where wet-mounting is not practical. Sensitive items like Cibachrome and Resin-Coated (RC) prints may be safely mounted in this manner. The procedure consists of transferring a film of pressure sensitive adhesive from a carrier sheet to the artwork and then to the mount board. This application is done with a hard plastic squeegee, with release paper placed between the art and the squeegee, working out from the centre to the edges. Pressure-sensitive adhesives come in sheets and rolls of various widths. The adhesive does not become "permanent" until pressure is applied, allowing repositioning of the item.

Peel-and-stick mount boards in mat board sizes are available in several thicknesses or layers. Pressure bonds the artwork to the mount board.

Dry Mounting

Dry mounting, also called "heat" mounting, uses tissue or film in rolls or sheets which are dry until heat is applied. In the case of the tissue, which has been coated on both sides with an adhesive substance (at the factory), the heat from the press activates the substance. Adhesive films are also activated by heat from the press. The film actually melts and

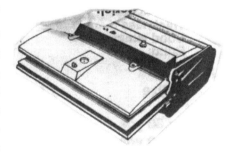

Dry mount Press

flows, forming the bond between the artwork and the mount board. Four factors enter into using the dry mounting systems.

1. **TIME** – the time it takes for the tissue or film adhesive to become activated and bond the art to the mount board. Upon removal from the press, the project must be placed under weights, such as a sheet of plate glass—which transfers the heat very rapidly, until cool.

2. **TEMPERATURE** – the adhesive manufacturer includes a schedule of recommended temperatures for tissues and films. Nevertheless, the type of art and how much heat it can "take" must be considered. Turning up the heat to speed up the process can end in disaster.

3. **HUMIDITY** – or the moisture content of both the art and the mount board is a factor to be considered. In order to ensure a complete bond the items should be pre-dried in the press.

4. **PRESSURE** – the lid or platen of the heat press contains the heating element. Once the press is up to the recommended heat, the art and its associated mounting components are placed under the platen and pressure is applied to ensure the bond will be sufficient.

Points to remember when dry mounting with heat:

- do not tack directly on the face of the artwork
- do not tack down the entire edge of the artwork
- do not make an "X" in the centre of the print
- do not tack all four corners of the print
- use release paper under and over the project
- set the heat and time
- when removing the item from the press place it under a weight such as plate glass to keep it flat while cooling down.
- see illustrations below.

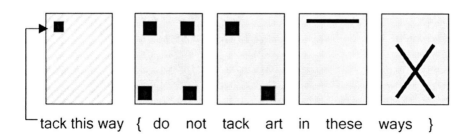

tack this way { do not tack art in these ways }

Putting together the components for dry mounting

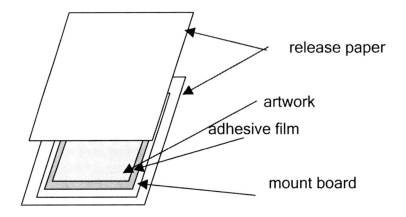

release paper

artwork

adhesive film

mount board

Dry Mount Press

There are three basic dry mount presses; one is a soft bed, another is a hard bed and the third is a hot/cold vacuum press.

1. The soft bed has a metal lid containing the heater elements; the lid clamps down compressing the art, adhesive material and the substrate. A thick sponge rubber pad is on the bottom plate. A thermostat controls the heat and a built-in timer regulates the time.

2. The hard bed press has a solid base and a rigid lid (platen) which contains the heating elements. The base, or bottom plate, is of cast metal with a thin, hard rubber pad. It has a timer and thermostat built into the lid to control the heat and the time it will be activated. Both models can handle oversize prints by doing them in sections, or "bites."

3. The combination hot/cold vacuum press has the heating elements in the lid, which can be made out of either a sheet of glass or a sheet of metal. It is thermostat and timer controlled. The limitation of this equipment is its size.

Papyrus—How to Mount

Handling this type of art requires some thought, especially in mounting. One thing is certain and that is to include the customer in your decisions. For methods in doing the actual work, consider:

1. The hinge or tab method, where you take a piece of conservation mat board slightly smaller than the art and with the use of mulberry hinges and conservation paste fasten the papyrus to the papyrus and then fold the hinges on to the mounting board (see illustrations).

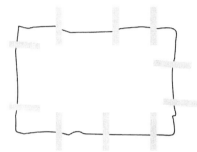

Hinges on the back of papyrus

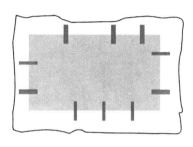

Hinges fold over mounting board

2. As an alternative, Dow Corning Silicone Rubber Sealer may be used to fasten the papyrus to the mounting board. Only small dabs of the adhesive are required. This adhesive is very strong and has the advantage of being removable. However, the customer must be informed as to potential problems if the procedure is to be reversed at some later date. Removing silicone from papyrus might also disturb some of the fibres.

3. Another option is to sew or stitch the papyrus on to the conservation board using thread that approximates the colour of the papyrus and taking tiny stitches. All of these methods assume the art is to be "floated," that is, raised above the mounting board. As in any framing project the customer should be involved, indicating that you, as the framer, are concerned about the their art.

CHAPTER TEN

Business Management

Introduction

"You've got to be careful if you don't know where you're going because you might not get there."

—Yogi Berra

In a survey of businesses with 20 or fewer employees:

- 19% indicated accounting and bookkeeping skills as their greatest weakness.
- 9% identified marketing as the most difficult task.
- 56% stated that 60 hours is the median work week.
- 63% took vacations on a regular basis.
- 54% did not have an advertising budget.
- 38% depended on word of mouth to get business.
- 21% used the Yellow Pages.

To be successful we must market our goods at a profit and still meet the expectations of our customers. If we satisfy the shopper but fail to make a profit we will soon be out of business. If we get the profit but fail to satisfy the shopper we will soon be out of customers. The secret of doing both depends on one word, **SERVICE.** Service means doing something so important for the customer that he or she is glad to pay a figure which permits us to make a profit.

Some common mistakes made by owners of small businesses, including picture framing shops, with a bit of advice on how to avoid them:

- mistaking your business for a hobby—be meticulous.
- trying to make your business all things to all people—become discriminating.
- attempting to start a business with too little cash—if necessary get a loan.
- unable to detect bad credit risks early—make sure you obtain a down payment.
- not pricing right for your products—ensure a profit but remain competitive.
- by developing a have-misgivings complex—seek help in making decisions.

The Business Plan

No frame shop, nor any business for that matter, can operate successfully without a business plan of some form. Whether it is jotted down on a piece of mat board, bound in a 20-page report, or somewhere in between you must have a plan—an organized way of putting your product and service ideas in motion. To do this, first you need some clear, realistic goals.

What is included in a business plan? Because the answer to that question is rather complex and requires serious thought, both financially and forecasting, it doubtless is the reason why many small businesses have not developed a business plan. A business plan takes time to work out.

What is a Business Plan?

A business plan is a recognized management tool used by successful and/or prospective businesses of all sizes to document business objectives and to propose how these objectives will be attained within a specific time period. It is a written document which describes who you are, what you plan to achieve, where your business will be located, when you expect to get under way, and how you will overcome the risks involved and provide the returns anticipated.

A business plan will provide information of your proposed venture to lenders, investors, and suppliers to demonstrate how you plan to use their money, and to establish a basis for credibility for your project.

The business plan should be prepared by the person who will be applying it—you. Outside assistance from consultants, accountants, bookkeepers, and experienced business people can definitely help, but you must draft the initial plan. After all, you are the one that is going to run the business once it is ready. After discussing it with others and listening to constructive criticism and advice, you may be required to modify your plan.

The substance of the business plan can be divided into three discrete parts:

1. Business Description.
2. Management Plan.
3. Financial Management Plan.

Business description

A. Details

- A precise description of your business; includes the legal aspects such as ownership, partnership or corporation; permits and licenses required.
- Type of business—retail market, service or production.
- Your product or service.
- Is the business new, buying an existing business, extension or franchise?
- Reasons how the business will be rewarding and possible growth potential.
- Schedule of business hours as well as days it will be open.
- Sources of research such as suppliers, banks, Chambers of Commerce and publications studied.

B. Type of Goods and Services

- Describe the advantages of your goods and services from your customers' viewpoint; what do your customers expect? Identify what it is you are selling and how this will, along with services, benefit your customers.

- Explain your cash flow plan.

- If you consider your product as unique, how does it differ from that of your competitors?

C. Location – the location should be easily identified, accessible and afford security.

- What type of space do you need?

- What makes the building, location and area easy to find and beneficial?

- Accessibility, public transportation and ample street lighting and parking are features that must be given serious consideration.

- What is the demographic history?

D. Marketing Plan – marketing plays a critical part in prosperous business enterprises.

- The foremost ingredient of an effective marketing plan is to know your clientele—their preferences, aversions, outlook and anticipation.

- Do a statistical demographic survey of your customers according to age, sex, estimated income, education and home.

- Outline clearly your market target.

- Are your sales stable, increasing or deteriorating?

- What about your market share, is it constant, growing or slipping?

- Does your market demand justify expansion?

- Have you decided on a pricing method, if so what is it?

E. The Competition – competition is in every facet of every day life.

- Business, whether based on the local level or on the global scale, is a highly competitive and variable domain; it is therefore advisable to know who your competitors are and how they operate.
- Who and where are your closest competitors and how are they doing?
- What about "associated" competitors, such as gift shops—who are they and where are they located?
- What have you discovered from their business activities and promotions?
- Do their merchandises and services compare with yours?

F. Basis for Pricing

- Develop a well-thought-out pricing and policy formula with periodic scrutinizing not only prices but also operating expenses to make sure that profits continue.
- Study your competitors' prices and adjust yours accordingly, but do not lose sight of the profit margin.

G. Promotion and Advertising

- The way you advertise your merchandise and services may well determine the success or failure of your business.
- Although it is very important to have premium goods and services, that is not enough; they must be advertised.
- It is not possible to stress too much the vital necessity for marketing since advertising and promotion are the principal means of communication for your business and should be regarded as such; design short, precise, clear wording that describes your goods and services, your location (with a map) and prices.
- The more serious attention you allocate to your marketing agenda the more prosperous your enterprise will be.

The Management (Administration) Plan

(Business Experience—what it takes)

- Operating a business cries out for more than simply the craving to be your own boss.
- Operating a business requires commitment, steadfastness, tact where other people are involved and the competence to manage finances.
- List your personal deficiencies and how you propose to remedy them.
- What or better who, comprise your management staff and have you prepared a job description for each one?
- Describe the salaries and benefits you are able to support at the outset.
- How are you going to hire and train the employees?

The Financial Management Plan

The Budget

- A realistic budget will tell you how much money you will need to start up your business and how much operating money you will need to keep it going.
- The start up budget will include licenses, equipment, lease, salaries, supplies, insurance, advertising, professional help (accountant, legal), utilities, renovations.
- The operating budget includes all of the above plus equipment depreciation, taxes and maintenance costs.
- The budget should include equipment and materials inventory, a statement of loan applications, a statement showing assets and liabilities, profit and loss, conventional income and cash flow projections.

Follow Up After Sales

After service attention is important. The service you provide leads to repeat customers, the most profitable kind to have.

Stay in touch with your clients. Set yourself apart by thanking them with a tangible reminder of how much you appreciate their business such as a coupon for a discount on their next purchase. Offer to stay open late if you sense your customer is on a deadline. And when that customer's major project or deadline is completed, follow up by remembering to ask how it went. And if a major customer makes a small request, do it for free when it is unexpected. *Remember, the cost of keeping a customer is small compared to the cost of finding a new one.*

Summary – the business plan:

- should contain the Cover Sheet, Statement of Intent and Table of Contents.
- should include supporting documents.
- should be specific when stating your goals.
- will assist you portray objectives, directions and strategies.
- provides information to gain investor confidence.
- will show your major suppliers your ability to pay.
- will convince potential customers of your ability to deliver.
- will tell you: – where you were.

    –where you are.

    –where you are going.

    –how you intend to get there.

Use your business plan at least quarterly to monitor your activities. Do not be afraid to make adjustments; today's business world is changing and so is yours.

Profit

a six letter word to keep in mind when doing business and ten points to help you remember

1. Ask for a deposit; people pick it up quicker; the pick up payment hurts less; if they put it on credit card they will likely pay for the whole thing instead of just a deposit, and this improves your cash flow.

2. In business you must increase your sales by 8% a year to stay even; never ask customers how much they want to spend; price is not the issue, design the piece and then talk cost; do not feel badly about your charges.

3. Do not sell "average;" start at the top and then, if necessary, work your way down; put expensive mat/frame samples on one corner and a less expensive combination on the opposite corner of the picture.

4. Do not try to please everybody, it is not possible, but: keep the walls "fresh;" move the pictures around from one location to another; no mark-down sales; get rid of old moulding stock by either making stock frames or giving it away.

5. Your counter should be kept clear for design consulting; limit the choices for the customer to two; do not place suggestions on all four corners of the picture; show your mat style ring binder.

6. Keep your samples clean and fresh; cut bevels on your mat board samples.

7. The business will not run itself, except downhill; you must consider your personal appearance, your hygiene and your attitude.

8. Advertise; doing business without advertising is like winking at a girl or boy, depending on preference, in the dark—only you know what you're doing; advertise to inform; advertise to educate what custom picture framing is; advertise to ensure name recognition; advertising should be about 6% of your gross income; in-store advertising—window display, sign, guest book, framed examples.

9. Opportunities are all around us; do not prejudge the customer's art as being cheap or of little value; it might have only sentimental

value, but this is important to the customer.

10. People expect to be waited on within 90 seconds after they enter your door; do not prejudge customers by the clothes they wear or their appearance.

Home-Based Business – The "Basement" Framer.

Introduction

Is a home-based business for you? This type of occupation is one of the fastest growing business structures in the Western World. One out of ten North Americans in the labour force now works at home, and studies suggest the total could reach 40 per cent early in this century. Equipped with affordable computers and communications technology, the home has been an effective and appealing workplace. Many home-based businesses are operated by homemakers or individuals experiencing a career change. Still others, such as retirees, people with physical disabilities and hobbyists have also found a profitable occupation potential in their homes.

Running a successful home-based business does not require a supernatural program, just a workable idea, common sense, commitment with self-discipline, and reliable advice. The more ready you are for the venture, however, the better.

One of the reasons why many home-based businesses start up is, if given the choice, the individuals involved prefer to stay small and manageable. The home setting, a familiar, comfortable and hospitable environment is, perhaps, sufficient reason to start up and remain at home. So, if your enterprise satisfies these and your financial expectations, it is quite possible that you may have the best of both worlds.

Picture Framing as a Home-Based Business

The home has proven to be a practical location to start and operate a picture framing business. Unfortunately, many home-based businesses struggle to survive. Being clear about your reasons for wanting a picture framing business in your home in the first place can lessen the struggle and help you make better performance decisions.

The matter of the home-based business comes up regularly in trade journals of every type, including picture framing. In the case of the home-based picture framer he/she is often viewed with disapproval by some store front picture framers. Others, especially those who are now "basement framers" (although many have converted part of their garages into very attractive framing studios) see this as a way of becoming established without the enormous overhead experienced by store owners. Many who started out in their homes have, before long, moved their businesses into malls or other retail facilities. Some equipment and material suppliers refuse to sell to operators who work out of their homes. But the debate does not diminish. The framer set on opening a framing business out of his/her home, must think it through very carefully.

Entrepreneurs, often known for their love of business and challenge associated with the "big risk" factor that agrees with starting a new business, include the home-based, self-employed business individuals although on a smaller scale. They start working from home for various reasons: economical, family considerations, commuting distances, lack of confidence in taking the "deep plunge," to name but a few. We all know that there are down sides to the home-based business. Among them are: the local license issuing authorities who impose restrictions such as signs and parking, if they will even permit a business to be run out of a home. For those living "under" the watchful eye of a strata council will find their business endeavours cramped by existing rules and by-laws of the residence; it might be difficult to get equipment and supplies. Your house is not a public area; in other words, the public does not have access to your place of business to the same extent that retail shops offer.

A case comes to mind while conducting a picture framing workshop in a remote community. One of the students asked the instructor, me, for my opinion on her basement set-up. We entered her house through the front door, took off our shoes, walked through the living room, dining room, kitchen and then down narrow basement stairs. Although the shop layout was adequate, the access resembled an obstacle course. It was difficult visualizing a customer navigating it with a large, framed print to be redone or picked up.

So, before you hang out your sign for your own business, try answering the following questions, honestly. Positive answers will indicate less time spent on the start up curve and a faster path to financial returns.

- Do you have proven credibility in this business? If the answer is "yes" it can help you secure those first important customers much faster than if you are unknown.

- Are you very good at what you do? If so, your first customers will assist your business to grow through word of mouth comments to their friends.

- Have you key contacts or know people who are able to send business your way? This is a wonderful way to start.

- What kind of cash reserves do you have going into a new enterprise? Specialists suggest that you should have saved at least six to twelve months' income before you venture out on your own.

According to a government agency on small business, the three primary causes of failure for businesses—and this might well apply to home-based outlets as well, are:

- Poor demand for the product in general or in your location.

- Lack of a business plan to control growth and measure business progress.

- Unrestricted overhead expenditures—poor business practices.

So, is home the best place? Consider the following possible advantages and shortcomings:

Possible Advantages
- Low risk of expensive mistakes.

- Opportunity to use household resources for business use.

- Low overhead and running costs.
- Progressive start up and growth.
- No commuting time or expense.
- Tax advantages with deductions allowed for use of part of the house.
- Relatively inexpensive way to test the market.
- Reduced child-care costs and increased quality time with the family.

Possible Limitations

- Isolation and lack of contact with colleagues.
- Increased family stress; the difficulty of separating business and family life.
- Need for self-discipline and the ability to plan and manage one's own time.
- By-laws and regulations affecting what you can and can not do in a home.
- Poor image—you may look more home-like than business-like.
- Conflict with neighbours over noise, traffic, and changed use of space.
- Parking problems.

Home-based businesses (framing galleries included) have their own characteristic challenges. The most apparent and of concern is the struggle between one's professional and personal lives. It takes family adjustments. Ground rules must be established such as the work place is off limits during the working day. Then there is the matter of isolation; some people thrive on this while others use formal and informal channels permitting home-based artisans to consider various business strategies, exchange ideas and keep in touch with the outside world through electronic means of communication such as the internet.

Plan for Opening a Home-based Business

It is believed by some people that all you need to start a business is a "good idea". While it is a "good idea" to have a good idea there is really quite a bit more to it than that. First of all one must decide which of three ways are most suitable for your home-based business:

A. Start from scratch, so to speak.

B. Buy an existing business and move it to your house.

C. Obtain a franchise.

A. Starting from Scratch

For many home-based operators, this is the only option. Household resources such as space, energy, time and materials can be used to help get the business established. This is especially important where finances are limited.

Starting from scratch requires more effort, time, and special skills than buying an existing business. It also involves more risks. It can take time for a new business to become known to prospective customers. The start up and development years can be times of modest income or even losses. Not all new business owners are ready to tackle the exacting demands that are entailed in a new business. Still, the compensations for those who prevail over the difficulties and keep at it can be boundless.

B. Buy an Existing Business (and move it to your home)

Buying an existing business is a way of getting into business. There are several advantages as well as drawbacks that differ from starting up a new business from scratch. Purchasing an existing business might reduce the time it takes for the investment to show a profit since it likely already has a customer base. Obtaining financing might be easier to get than a business without a track record.

Frequently neither new proprietors nor new financing can improve an unsound business. Before entering into transactions to purchase the business study the business plan and discuss the proposition with your lawyer, accountant and banker.

C. Buying a Franchise

Although franchises are not common for home-based businesses, they are present. Purchasing a franchise entails buying the rights and backing systems to own and operate a business that has been designed by someone else. With a franchise you buy a piece of something already firmly incorporated. So, on the one hand this means you will have to do things someone else's way but on the other hand business systems are laid out for you and, in most cases, support is available.

The best advice, as with all opportunities, is to do your research carefully. Talk with a few franchisees who can tell you what it is really like being part of the franchise in which you are interested.

Summary

- Are you a self-starter? Thriving business operators are on the go, they do not wait for the phone to ring, they are disciplined and do not yield to distractions.

- Have you a positive outlook? This is vital since you will experience highs and lows.

- How do you view competition, as a challenge or as the "enemy"? The rivalry should not be viewed as the foe but rather as a challenge to assert your place in the market share.

- Are you willing to work long hours? Late nights, long days, forfeit holidays are often "part of the game," especially in the start up phase.

- Have you the resources to adapt your everyday life? Making ends meet without a secure income is in itself a challenge.

- Are you self-disciplined and persevering? Being self-employed requires keeping deadlines, assuming heavy workloads and incorporating competent managerial skills.

Too often, when buying a picture framing business including the building, little or no attention is paid to the condition of the foundation or roof. An enthusiastic real estate broker quite often tips the scales in favour of the purchaser's decision.

Management Consultants

The merit of sound counsel

In his early days of operating a picture framing shop/gallery the author had an opportunity to purchase a building, "just perfect" for a gallery in the centre of the business district of his city. His offer to purchase had been accepted by the building's owner and now it remained to get the required down payment and arrange the financing. The loans officer at the bank where his business and personal accounts were located requested to see his business plan. An appointment was made for the following day. That evening he, after procuring several books on business plans from the library, spent quite a few hours drawing up a business plan, which in his estimation was somewhat of a masterpiece.

The appointment the following day did not last long. The loans officer said on the basis of that plan no loan was possible. Somewhat disheartened, he went to the federal government business bank, an institution established to help small businesses. The manager looked at the business plan, furrowed his brow, a not-too-encouraging sign, and said, "Man, you don't need a loan, you need counselling." So he was assigned a management consultant who, having been the president of one of the largest department store chains in Canada, had some sound and, at times, hard to take suggestions. The sessions resulted in a financial turn around for the business. The building purchase plan was abandoned. In business as in life, good advice is much like good medicine, you know it will help you and yet it is, at times, hard to swallow. (As an aside, the building in question is now worth well over a million dollars.)

Statistics show that 80 per cent of businesses disappear within five years of opening, so looking for dependable advice could be the solution in your start-up phase, what your business presently needs or what will keep it vigorous in the days ahead. These dismal data along with a very competitive commercial world have motivated more and more business owners to search for the assistance of management consultants. In fact these services are becoming increasingly in high demand. Consultants draw on their own business experiences and their ability to assist businesses in such areas as management, sales development, critical planning, start up essentials and future considerations.

Management consultants are hired for short-term and long-term assignments. Fees vary with the magnitude of the project and the duration of the contract. In very small businesses, the manager (usually the owner) may not have the skills necessary to fulfil a particular business phase demand. Frequently, entrepreneurs start businesses with skills in certain areas but they do not necessarily include management competence. Management consultants make fine adjustments to the enterprise, but unless their counsel is acted upon or if you do not have confidence in their advice, money spent on the consultations is money not well-spent.

Getting into business is costly both in a financial sense but also as a personal investment. Business owners and managers seek to avoid costly blunders while pursuing success and development. Management consultants are key "ingredients" in the process.

Bad Debts—reduce the risk

People starting in a service industry are often more interested in carrying out their work than in forming and instituting an easily understood credit and invoicing policy. Many new business owners/managers have had a minimal amount of business experience, some have had none. They are not aware of the problems that can arise. But having a strategy in place that works is imperative to your survival. It takes only a few bad debts to either wipe out the profits for a whole year or put your company out of business altogether.

There are, however, some useful procedures worthy of attention to reduce the risk of bad debts. They might not suit every occasion, but consider:

Have a clear understanding on fees to be charged. Verbal discussions are followed by a written work order. Although many people feel uncomfortable discussing money matters, it is unavoidable to ensure that you will get the amount of money you anticipate for the service provided. To make certain that no confusion occurs, follow up your discussion with your customer by preparing a work order followed with a detailed invoice.

The down payment. Customers should be asked for a deposit or down payment. The amount would likely vary with the track record of the customer or according to the amount of material required to complete the work ordered. The customary amount is fifty per cent of the total invoice or at least enough to cover the materials purchased for the project. This is also an effective method for safeguarding your business from a new patron who might not pay promptly or one who would rather not pay at all.

Overdue payments. When you see that an invoice is past due by more than a week, set your collection procedure to work at once.

To summarize, in our type of business as in most small businesses, you are it. You are the person on which the success of the enterprise depends. You are the organizer, the producer of the goods and services offered the appraiser, the promoter and the wearer of many more hats associated with your business, including that of bill collector. The business is your livelihood. Involve the customer in the work you are doing by making him/her cognizant of your skills, experience, benefits and services. By so doing you are bringing them into the "picture" and are likely to reduce the risk of bad debts.

First Impressions

At a recent seminar on operating a small business, the matter of gaining customer confidence came up as a topic for discussion. Dress "code" and appearance were high on the list for attention.

We have all heard it countless times: *you only get one chance to make a first impression.* Yet, many otherwise skilled workers lose customer trust because of the way they dress or the way they appear. Experts suggest you should think carefully about who you are going to meet during the day. How you dress makes a significant impression. Of course in an age of liberal behaviour and self-expression regarding styles and appearances, this suggestion is not popular. However, fair or otherwise, first impressions are usually lasting impressions.

There is more than clothes to be taken into account, especially personal grooming. This means having tidy, well-kept hair, clean hands including fingernails, and no smoking in the workplace. Managers and employees should be aware that in sales, skills, although important, are supplemented by "image". In the market-place it matters a great deal.

Several years ago the author sold his framing gallery to a recent immigrant. In his former culture it appeared that it was permissible to smoke in the workplace, so he kept it up in spite of counsel to the contrary. In fact, within a short period of time there were cigarette butts and burns everywhere—even on the mat cutter base! To top it off, the atmosphere reeked of stale smoke. After the agreed-to transition/tutoring period was over the author left with a degree of apprehension. Within two years his business closed. From reports it is believed that his smoking obsession in his workplace was a contributing factor.

Besides good service, the public expects cleanliness. There is no question but that being well-dressed and well-groomed will contribute to your self-confidence and to the trust of your customers.

Framing gallery/shop owners who have complementary items such as pottery, crafted jewellery and stained glass articles say that these objects draw in customers who generally would not find anything they liked or could afford.

When Thinking Of Financial Support, Think BIG

Some small business owners, when approaching a bank for a loan or line of credit feel like an army private walking into the commanding general's office seeking a favour. But small business is very important for the big banks and they know it. There is no need to approach them with cap in hand. However, to help strike a deal to your needs have a sound business plan and do some critical comparison bank shopping. Inform them that you intend to move your mortgage, line of credit, retirement investments, and personal loan to the bank that provides the best business arrangement.

Present a confident image. Banks need you, so do not be afraid to ask for all the financing you require. And by no means put up your house as security for your business. Expect the bank to provide the finances you ask for and do not be easily deterred. Frequently if one branch turns you down another branch of the same bank will see things your way.

If repayments are too high ask to have them rescheduled. This is done all the time for large corporations so it is nothing new to the banks, so do not be afraid to ask. Taking a friend along, especially someone with financial knowledge often helps your case since bank loan employees do not like to present a negative image especially in front of witnesses.

Summary

1. Know your business plan inside out.

2. Ask around for the name of an understanding account manager.

3. Compare rates at different banks.

4. Use mortgage and retirement investments to bargain for better terms.

5. Take the full amount of credit available to you.

6. Ask for rescheduling of loan payments if needed.

7. Ask for dispute resolution if disagreements arise.

CHAPTER ELEVEN

Marketing

When you have decided what business you are in—picture framing, you have made your first marketing decision. Successful marketing starts with the owner-manager. You have to know your products and services and the expectations of your customers.

When you pick a site to locate your business, consider the nature of your service. For example, if you pick up and deliver you will want a location where the travel time is low. On the other hand, if the customer must come to your shop the site must be conveniently located and easy to find. You must pick the site that offers the best possibilities of being profitable. When choosing an area, consider the following:

- Population and growth potential.
- Income, age, occupation of the population.
- Number of competitive services in and around your proposed location.
- Local ordinances and zoning regulations.
- Type of business traffic in your area—commercial, residential, seasonal.

The local chamber of commerce can help you with these details.

Promotion and Advertising

In spite of the fact that advertising and marketing in the last decade have become somewhat complicated, as a retail custom framer you need to be aware of the various media available for your use and which you must employ.

Marketing is *all the things* you do to promote your business. Marketing starts at the time when you visualize which products and services you will offer to potential customers when they begin to deal with your business on a *regular* basis. Note the words "all the things" and "regular," they are significant.

Your Image

How many times have you seen a business sign, a telephone directory or a delivery vehicle with a catchy name for some company with no reference in the name as to what they do? Does your business have a name that clearly communicates what your product or service is? For example, what does Dorset Gallery convey? Is it a furniture gallery, a shooting gallery, art gallery or a floor covering emporium? Do not require your potential customers to guess at what goes on in your work place. With a sign that says:

Metro **Picture Framing** *Gallery*

"guess work" is eliminated. The attention is immediately drawn to what you do. All the advertising you do will be wasted if the name of your company and its logo do not announce a distinct image. Association and repetition are keys to successful advertising.

Although the above are but suggested sketches which a graphic artist would "flesh" out, note the uniformity in the address and advertisement size. The standard size and the repetition is what will catch the eye of the reader.

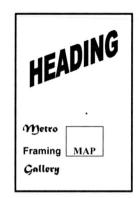

- **REPETITION REPETITION REPETITION**
- **EYE-CATCHING HEADLINES**
- **STRESS the BENEFITS**
- **Brevity IN COPY**

Make up a series of 4 or 5 ads each one featuring a specialty such as framing needlework, objects, antique or fragile art restoration, and other areas of expertise.

Some of the questions to consider are:
- Does the name of my business clearly state what I do?
- Is my business name easily recognized and remembered?
- Is it always printed in the same type style on all my office supplies?
- Is my logo easily recognized by my customers?
- Do I answer the phone with the name of my company?

Your ads must clearly depict what you are "selling":
- We market well-known brands and accredited artists' works.
- Our guiding principle is service.
- Our frame selection is one of the largest in town.

- The location of our gallery offers free parking.
- Come in and discuss our free home and office enhancement services.
- We offer frame-it-yourself education classes.
- Our estimates are concise and free.
- One of our specialties is commercial business.
- Call us for in-home or in-office estimates.
- All our framing is done "in-house."

Who are your customers?

- Those that need your framing services and merchandise.
- Those who are presently seeking out your services and merchandise.
- Those who can afford framing services and merchandise.

Standards that your customers expect:

- **Quick and courteous service;** most people are in a hurry; long queues deter people from "hanging around;" acknowledge people as they come into your gallery, it builds good will and projects a favourable image.
- **Sufficient supplies;** advertising products and services you are unable to deliver wastes your money; making a habit of running short of goods results in customers losing confidence in you.
- **Pricing;** prices clearly and appropriately marked gains customer confidence in your integrity; if products are not priced customers may well wonder the reason for this.
- **Refund process;** make replacements or refunds to your customers readily and willingly; remember the image you are trying to project.
- **Be truthful;** integrity is the basis of good business.
- **Customer observations;** when you enter your shop in the morning, as the first customer might look around; are the displays exciting, the windows clean, are the aisles ample and neat?
- **Telephone courtesy;** telephone manners of you and your staff signify the type of service customers can expect from your establishment.

Work habits that your customers do not tolerate

- **High pressure approach;** a confident, low-key approach rather than an aggressive attitude will result in more sales for you.

- **Promises not kept;** these produce nothing but grief for store managers and customers soon know if you can be trusted, so be truthful.

- **Messy environment;** slovenly store appearance implies careless accounting, indifferent sales approaches and mediocre work; this view ruins your image.

- **Shoddy packaging;** nothing will cause a customer to blow up more than to have their package from your shop come apart in public.

Which marketing strategy is best for you?

- If it is newspaper advertising; the local weekly newspaper is preferred.

- If it is writing "picture framing" articles; present them to the local newspaper.

- If it is designing and distributing a regular newsletter; include sales specials.

- If it is advertising in business magazines; reach your corporate customers.

- If it is direct mail; include letters, brochures and circulars.

- If your emphasis is placed in the Yellow Pages; have it listed under appropriate headings.

- If it is flyers; limit them to the start up period to introduce your frame shop to the community.

- Then there are others; radio, TV, store signs, vehicle signs, artists' shows.

What is the budget price tag for advertising

"Will my investment in advertising really pay off?" is a common question. Advertising consultants can give you countless "pay off" testimonials in answer to that question. The follow-up question might well be, "How much should I spend in advertising to produce the volume of sales I need to be profitable?"

Again, advertising or marketing consultants have several methods for arriving at a figure to fit into your budget. Two approaches most often used are:

- Per cent of Sales Method
- Function or Task Method

The per cent of sales method has two beneficial features: one, it is simple, and two, it is not difficult to control. It is simple because government statistics show that retail store advertising falls in the 2.5% to 4% range of the gross sales, so then if your annual gross sales volume is $250,000, your advertisement budget would lie in the $6,250 to $10,000 range and if your annual gross volume of sales happened to be $100,000, your advertising budget would range from $2,500 to $4,000. Since these are only guidelines, you would need to decide how much you can spend on advertising.

The control aspect of this method provides you with a great degree of flexibility. The picture framing business is affected by certain periods throughout the year such as Valentine's Day, Mother's Day, Father's Day, graduations, and Christmas to name a few. You have the flexibility to increase your advertising expenditure prior to these special periods.

The task method process is one where you examine your short-term and long-term objectives and merely set aside the amount you believe will satisfy the task or the objective. The danger with this method is that many retail managers are inclined to view this budget item as no more important than some mundane store housekeeping chore. Consider advertising as an investment in the future success of your gallery.

The task method, although it is not as meticulous as the per cent method, if thoughtfully planned, can be beneficial in deciding how much of the budget should be spent on marketing.

It is more profitable to sell one $150 custom frame order than three $50 frame projects.

Window Display

Your store windows introduce your frame shop to the public. Based on the message your display sends, the public develops an impression of your frame shop even before they walk inside. Your windows should convey the quality, style, and distinctiveness of your store.

What have you done with Aunt Helen's spoon collection, with your reward ribbons, with your daughter's first dress, with your son's first pair of shoes? Most of us have souvenirs, mementos, keepsakes and heirlooms tucked away in a dresser, desk drawer or on a shelf. For every item you can think of in your drawers or closets, you can bet that your customers have one too. To display these "silent sellers" on your gallery walls or in your display windows will bring in framing jobs without a word from you. Establish an attractive display area. Become creative with matting variations, shadow box frames and multiple mat openings.

Windows are among the most effective marketing tools in the retailer's toolkit. The window is the "public face" of the shop, whether it is a large or small shop, and this applies particularly to the picture framing industry. If you make it striking or pertinent to a season or other topic, there is a potential for bringing customers into your store. It need not be expensive, complex or ornate. Simple and creative concepts are often most noted.

Visual merchandising sells products. If a store appears dull and uninteresting, the public will pass right by. As a book is often judged by its cover, so a store is often judged by its appearance and the window is this "appearance."

You should look to attract people who do not frequent your establishment. These are the people who could be in the market to buy a framed print if they are sufficiently motivated, or have an old photograph or portrait at home needing to be restored and framed. Your window display could be the catalyst needed to remind them of what they have that still needs attention. Your regular customers are already familiar with your skills but they need to be excited by your new innovations and products. These are best displayed in your window.

Improve Awareness

Not only should you expect to generate sales, but also initiate a much greater awareness for your business. The creativity you show in a tasteful window display will enhance the perception for a business which should be seen as having skilful and refined abilities.

Do not forget the competition especially if you are one of several framing galleries in the area. Although it is difficult to gauge, the "relaxed ambience" should not be disregarded when customers enter your establishment.

Low-priced Alternatives

You may think you are unable to afford it. There are companies around that specialize in dressing windows, but they are generally used by the large department stores. For the smaller shop or gallery there are alternatives such as:

- Doing it yourself; design, construct and decorate it yourself
- Get some "outside" assistance; there are freelancers in every enterprise including this one.

As with any promotional project, you must decide what your objectives are because that will affect the types of window displays you will need. Consider:

- To market a certain product such as a new moulding, a new type of glass or a new technique for framing needle art.
- To reinforce a certain image; "expensive looking is not necessarily expensive buying," "your art deserves the best craftsmanship."
- To make the public aware of special promotions.
- To promote local events.

Once you have determined what it is you want to accomplish with the window display, you can then set about to try your hand at it.

Frugal Framers

When it comes to window displays some framers are inclined to be unduly cautious, likely thinking that nothing should detract from work done behind the scenes. Good displays will actually enhance the art and not depreciate it. So, if you have not already decided on the style you want your window to convey, do it soon. People are rather careful of how they spend their discretionary money, and to make the wisest choices they are window shopping.

According to one professional window dresser with regard to window displays in smaller shops and galleries, the shortcomings frequently are:

- Infrequent change – shopkeepers often do not bother changing their displays. From one month to the next; before long it becomes a boring scene.

- Failure to clean – windows get dusty and dirty very quickly.

- Untidy – there are shopkeepers who clutter up the window; a single portrait or print can make its own statement.

- Lighting – keep the spotlights trained on the object you want to feature; remember to use non-reflective glass with pictures, and do not forget to replace burned out bulbs.

- Making do – some shop operators resent spending money on their windows, but you must spend money to make money; the materials purchased for your display can be used again.

- Bewildering – framers have been known to place moulding and mat board corner samples in the window as a display; people have a difficult time visualizing how they would look on their art so the chances of stimulating their imaginations are minimal.

Summary – Display Your Abilities

Window displays are attention-getters. This type of marketing is very effective especially to promote seasonal events, special occasions such as announcing the presence of visiting artists and new pictures or frames. Suggestions for your consideration:

- Settle on what you want to feature—a new artist, a new product line.

- Make a sketch of how you want the window to appear.

- Gather the items you want to display in the window; you may be able to borrow props from gift shops or antique stores.

- Location of the items in the window; items with greatest selling potential up front; like items grouped together at eye level; arrive at a balanced look.

- Keep the display fresh; change items on display frequently, at least every four weeks.

- The human eye can absorb only so much in one pass; you are trying to achieve one outcome; a lot of "things" in the window lead to bewilderment.

- Employing a colour motif is useful in directing the observer to take in the whole window display, but avoid using a mixed bag of colours by sticking to either the primary colours or pastels.

- Keep the display simple; two or three items might be enough to emphasize your point.

- Try to achieve one objective with each display; perhaps framed portraits one time, framed certificates the next, followed by needle art and then limited edition prints.

Sell the customer what they want, not what you want to sell.

Trade Shows – Promoting Your Business

Picture framers have always had a concern deciding which are the most effective methods for promoting their businesses. The ever-increasing costs related to direct sales, combined with the inability to effectively monitor their returns on investment have forced companies to look at new and innovative ways to publicize what they do. Trade shows, as a form of marketing, have grown into one of the most effective ways of meeting the challenge.

As with any business expenditure, trade show marketing is an investment and, as such, should be carefully appraised. All shows are not equal. Costs can escalate when you consider direct expenses, such as booth fees, signs, promotional material, and indirect expenses, such as lost production time, travelling and parking charges. One good show, however, can generate enough customers and create orders that more than justify the cost.

How can you tell which show has enough potential value and demands taking part? Where and how are you going to obtain the most benefits in terms of contacts and sales? You might want to consider the following points in appraising a trade show:

Show direction – what is the show mandate; is it in line with your business objectives and is it designed to attract your target market?

Sponsors – who are the sponsors of the show and do they add prestige and credibility to the event?

Industry scheduling – are there other industry related events scheduled around the date of the show and do they present a possible conflict to your company or to potential show attendees?

Show planning – is the show attractive to attendees in terms of location, hours, parking, and are there special incentives to attend?

Advertising – how is the show to be promoted and advertised, and when is the promotion scheduled to start?

Floor layout – how inviting is the show, and can all exhibitors be assured of walk-by traffic; can exhibitors choose their own space?

Attendance tracking – will show organizers provide exhibitors with a list of attendees for follow-up marketing?

Exhibitor base – what type of exhibitors does the show usually attract and are direct competitors taken into consideration when determining layout?

Planning for slack periods – have show organizers scheduled demonstrations and draws for slack or quiet periods?

Show management – what are the credentials of those who are managing the event and can they assure a successful show in terms of attendance and management, and provide exhibitors with the opportunity of generating the return on investment they are looking for?

Summary

There are many reasons for exhibiting but your objectives must be clear and they might include:

- Producing orders.
- Assembling first-rate leads.

- Creating direct sales.
- Presenting a new product; exchanging information with dealers and company representatives.
- Making available a press release to the media.

You must avoid having too many objectives. Select one or two key focus areas and make them measurable. Having detectable objectives will give your purposes real direction.

Computer Technology

The person who takes on the operation of a small business quickly finds out that the computer is as vital a part of his or her business as the telephone, filing cabinet, typewriter, cash register, calculator and even the cheque-book. The fact is that the computer is doing all of those things and more, all in one small box.

Small business and the computer are perfectly suited to each other. Small business has the same problems as big business but on a more personal level. These include marketing, shortage of reliable employees, tax implementation and revisions, inventory control and constant technological changes. The computer can assist you in all these potential problem areas.

A computer will help you work more productively and free your most valuable asset—time; time to evaluate your product or service; time to plan ahead; time to read and think; time to bring in new methods and ideas. All or any of these are reason enough to get and use a computer.

A computer can do many things for your business. You will need to decide which jobs you want your computer to do. You can buy off-the-shelf programs to deal with point-of-sale invoices, inventory control, accounts receivable and payable, ledgers and journals, sales analyses and scheduling. You do not have to know how to program.

The key thing is to know what programs are available and to appraise them to see which will deliver the best of what you require in terms of cost and performance. Competent computer sales people can help you with this. Once the computer is installed you will soon see the considerable benefits it offers.

CHAPTER TWELVE

Pricing

An average of just over 74% of picture framers, in a survey conducted in eight regions researched, earned eight dollars or less per hour. The findings were all the more troubling considering that the figures included owners of the businesses. Surely the knowledge, skills and responsibilities of a custom framer are worth more than those of a cleaner or a fast foods employee.

Another survey looked at the prices charged for three different framing jobs against specific sizes, qualities and materials. The findings revealed that 60% of framers were charging below average, some well below, with a further 9.4% charging around the average. Add those two percentages together and we find a figure not far removed from that of very low earners in the first survey. It is not difficult to suspect a strong connection between prices charged and earnings.

There are those who believe that earnings are related to marketing. However, marketing can only bring about the right results if one's prices are right to start with. But what is the right price?

Any business school will teach that the *right price* is that which is right for both the customer and the merchant. There is nothing wrong with that theory. It is clear then that the customer's idea of *right price* can be based not on knowledge of production costs but on the *price expectation* which in turn is based on what one has become accustomed to paying. So, if it costs a framer $60.00 to produce a given type of framing job and he is foolish enough to sell it on a regular basis for $40.00, he will convince his customers that $40.00 is the r*ight price*. In fact, he will have conditioned his customers to a "price expectancy."

If you are doing plenty of work but are not making enough money, then there is something wrong with your prices and you will need to ask yourself, "just who is it that decides the price of my framing?" If we think about the question and answer it honestly, we may find ourselves forced to admit that our previous excuses such as *market influences, that twit down the street being cheaper, customer spending power, start to sound a bit weak.*

Pricing Practices

Despite the many bizarre and in some cases, wonderful pricing methods put to use by framers, they essentially boil down to two main systems:

1. suppliers' price for materials X multiplier = Selling Price.

2. cost of materials + time taken X mark-up = Selling Price. It is this method which pricing seeks to address; many small business managers and picture framers fit into this category. They might have great skills in their craft but are less proficient when it comes to dollars and cents. The bank routine when one seeks financial help is to give the applicant a fistful of coloured brochures which seem more appropriate for a large corporation than for someone producing one-of-a-kind custom frames. It makes one wonder whether some banks really know what small business is. Seminars on business skills often do little more than recommend that one "charges" what the market will bear.

How to Price

When managing a retail business such as custom picture framing you must consider all costs including the <u>wholesale cost of materials, labour, utilities, advertising, lease, mark-up</u> and many more. In fact the final financial review must show that:

Retail (Selling) Price minus [Real Cost (wholesale cost + shipping + wastage + cost of maintaining inventory) + Labour Cost (includes operating costs)] = **NET PROFIT**

When establishing retail prices for your goods and services several factors come into play; these include:

- **real or total cost of materials** (wholesale price + shipping charges, around 5% + waste factor, around 20% + inventory costs [money tied up in inventory] roughly 2%).

- **mark-up** (customarily 2.5 times; this applies equally to custom-made, ready-made and gift items).

- **labour** (shop charge per hour includes employees' salaries and benefits; but also includes overhead costs such as lease, utilities, advertising, insurance, telephone, attending trade shows and bank charges).

To calculate shop charges take your annual operating costs which include salaries, benefits and overhead costs, then divide this by the total labour hours. If you are starting out and do not have an annual record, estimate what costs and total hours might be. Your business plan should help you here. For example, if your costs were $90,000 for the past year (or estimated) and labour hours for the same period were 5,000 then:

$90,000 ÷ 5,000 = $18 per hour; therefore your shop charges are 18 X 2.5 (mark-up) = **$45 per hour**

The Basic Formula

ACTUAL COST X MARK-UP + LABOUR = SELLING PRICE

ACTUAL COST is the cost from the vendor + other associated costs such as:

- freight to your shop.
- waste or shrinkage (scraps, mistakes, liberated (stolen)) 15% to 20%.
- carrying costs (loss of interest)—inventory stock, approximately 3%.

MARK-UP commonly 2X to 2.5X.

LABOUR includes:

- the time it takes to produce an item using shop rate (not employees' rate).
- employees' labour rate plus benefits.
- shop rate (overhead—rent, light, utilities, heat, insurance, advertising); to calculate shop rate look at the operating expenses for your 12-month period, divide this by the number of hours you are open in the year. For example, operating expenses are $100,000, hours open are 2,500 so the shop charge is 100,000 divided by 2,500 = $40 per hour ($30/hour is common).

Pricing Moulding

Remember the formula: Actual Cost X mark-up + labour = Selling Price. So,

Cost + Freight + Waste + Carrying Costs = **Actual Cost**
100% + 8% + 20% + 3% = **131%**

If the mark-up is 2.5 and your **Actual Cost** is 131% of the product cost, consider this formula:

Actual Cost X mark-up = adjusted mark-up 131% X 2.5 = **327.5%** **or 3.275 times**

This becomes the mark-up figure you will use in the pricing formula for manufactured goods.

Labour

- First of all calculate how long it takes (average) to build a frame; for example, assume it takes 15 minutes (¼ hour) to cut and join the frame.
- Labour charge per frame is derived by multiplying this figure by the shop's hourly rate—$40/hour.
- Cost of moulding is expressed in feet, and if we are using 5.5 feet as an   average footage per frame, then: (labour charge X time) ÷ average frame = ($40 X ¼) ÷ 5.5 = $1.82 per foot.

(labour charge X time) ÷ average frame = labour charge per foot

($40 X ¼)   ÷   5.5   = $1.82 per foot

This gives us a labour charge that can be added to the marked-up cost of the moulding. The retail price of moulding with an invoice cost of 50¢ per foot would be multiplied by the adjusted mark-up of 3.275 and add a labour charge of $1.82.

(.50/ft X 3.275) + $1.82 = Selling Price per foot
$1.64 + $1.82 = $3.46 per foot

Mat board

The pricing formula works with mat board and other products such as glass. You will need to do some research to find your accurate figures.

You can make a pricing chart for mat board by deciding what part of a full sheet you will require for specific sizes of mats such as 8" X 10" or 11" X 14"

Sizes	8" X 10"	11" X 14"	16" X 20"	20" X 24"
United Inches	18	25	36	44

Now you calculate the percentage of a full sheet that is needed for each size. For example, an 8" X 10" mat has an area of 80 square inches. A 32" X 40" mat board has an area of 1,280 square inches. So then we produce the following chart:

UI	(8 X 10)18	(11 X 14)25	(16 X 20)36	(20 X 24)44
Area (square inches)	80	154	320	480
% of full sheet	6.25	12.03	25	37.5

Figuring out the **Actual Cost** of a sheet of mat board using our formula (see above) and assuming a mat board price of $9.50, we have:

Cost	+	Freight	+	Waste	+	Carrying Cost	=	Actual Cost
100%	+	12%	+	20%	+	2%	=	134%
$9.50	+	1.14	+	1.90	+	0.19	=	$12.73

This means that a mat board which was sold to you for $9.50 and adding the various additional costs **actually** costs you $12.73.

Now consider the mark-up amount of 2.5. In our example the formula is 134% X 2.5 = 335% or times 3.35.

So, a full sheet of mat board provides a selling price of:

Cost   x adjusted mark-up = Selling Price
$9.50 x 3.35   = $31.825 or **$31.83**

Now we must determine the selling price for each size on the chart using an arbitrary figure of $9.00 for labour (finding the mat board, cutting the blank to size, cutting the opening, marking and returning the pieces left over to stock).

Therefore in a 20" X 24" mat we have an area of 480 square inches or 37.5% of a full sheet, so the formula is:

Percentage x cost of full sheet + labour = Selling Price for 20" X 24" mat

(0.375 X $31.83) + $9.00 = Selling Price

$11.93 + $9.00 = $20.93 – the Selling Price

United Inches	18	25	36	44
Mat Selling Price	$10.99	$12.84	$16.96	$20.93

A similar chart can be developed for glass.

Financial Profits Should Be Fundamental

Your charges must cover:

- cost of goods.
- expenses.
- your profit.

It is important to not deceive yourself:

- know why your prices are at their current level.
- check your prices at least three times a year.
- maintain a price that is fair to your customer and yet assures your profitability.

Once you have decided on the prices you need to charge to make a profit, and these prices vary from region to region, it is a good plan to construct an easy-to-read chart similar to the example below.

A Retail Price Sheet – per United Inch (UI)

Mat Board

Regular	.24
Conservation	.45
Colour Core	.47
Fabric (Suede)	.55

Glass

Regular	.27
Reflection Control	.45
Conservation	.47

Mounting Board

Regular - Acid-Free	.18
Foam Board - Regular (1/8")	.22
Foam Board - Acid-Free (1/8")	.30

Services

    Mounting - Regular, including the board   .27

    Mounting - Conservation - including hinges   .64

    Laminating   .35

    Shrink Wrapping   .28

    Fitting   .26

    Stretching - Canvas, including stretcher frame .65

    Stretching - Needlework, including board   .75

Moulding

    Code A   1.10

    Code B   1.30

    Code C   1.40

    Code D   1.50

    Code E   1.60

United Inches	18	25	30	36	42	48
Mats (including one opening):						
Conservation	8.10	10.50	12.00	14.00	15.20	17.00
Regular	4.00	5.20	6.50	7.90	8.40	10.50
Fabric (suede)	13.50	18.00	22.50	23.40	27.30	29.85
Mounting Board:	1.44	1.92	2.70	2.88	3.78	4.32
Foam Board (acid free)	4.50	6.00	7.50	9.00	10.30	12.40
Foam Board (regular)	3.60	7.10	8.70	11.00	12.10	13.90
Glass:						
Conservation (clear)	17.10	22.80	28.50	34.20	39.90	45.60
Reflection Control	12.60	16.80	21.00	25.20	29.40	33.60
Regular	4.50	6.00	7.50	9.00	10.50	12.00
Mounting:						
Regular (including board)	3.96	5.28	6.60	7.92	9.24	10.56
Conservation (hinges)	14.60	16.53	18.10	21.90	22.70	26.10
]Stretching:						
Oil (including stretcher bars)	14.40	16.55	20.15	23.05	26.65	30.95
Needlework (including board	14.40	16.55	20.15	23.05	26.65	30.95
Fitting	4.50	6.00	7.50	9.00	10.50	12.00
Fillets	10.80	15.00	18.00	21.60	25.20	28.80
Laminating	5.55	6.50	7.50	12.15	15.30	17.80
Shrink Wrap	4.50	6.00	7.50	9.00	10.50	12.00
Moulding:						
metal	17.10	22.90	28.75	32.40	38.20	45.15
wood - per UI	Code 3 - 1.00 Code 4 - 1.10 Code 5 - 1.25 Code 6 - 1.35 Code 7 - 1.50 Code 8 - 1.75 Code 9 - 2.00 Code 10 - 2.25.					

J. Edwin Warkentin

CHAPTER THIRTEEN

The Work Order

Taking in the customer's order is a very important part in operating a frame shop. The work order form which, in reality, is a contract between the customer and you is also the reference form to which you and your employees will adhere from the time the customer leaves the order until the customer picks it up or has it delivered. It is the customer's assurance that the item will be cared for in a professional way and it is your protection, especially if <u>completely</u> filled out, in case of a claim. All damages relating to the art should be noted on the order form. Point out the irregularities on the item and have the customer sign the order.

You will need to determine what services you are offering, such as various types of mats, glass, moulding, mounting, liners, fillets, stretching canvas and needlework, conservation and "other." The order form itemizes each component of the framing project along with the total price. You are selling a complete unit so it is not a good policy to inform the customer that you are charging $8.50 for a piece of glass that might be obtainable at a glass shop for $3.50, and $12.00 for a mat when a whole sheet may be bought for $13.50. Your mark-up takes care of the overhead and shop operating expenses.

The work order form's function is to record and organize all the information pertaining to each framing job in a concise, regulated way. Use the 3-copy form with a copy for the customer, one goes with the order and the other for ordering supplies. To summarize what appears on the order form:

- Irregularities; note damaged or soiled areas of the art.
- The framing elements and sizes; write clearly and completely.
- Manner of payment; always request a down payment.
- Show pick-up date; make sure it is ready on that date.
- Today's date; the date the order was received.
- Your company name, address and telephone number.
- Customer's name, address, telephone number and signature.
- Description of customer's order.
- Disclaimer; if the customer does not want conservation method of framing used.
- Not liable for order if it is left for an extended period without prior arrangement. The above summary items are important and should be included. The following Illustration is an example of what a complete work order should look like.

Name of Frame Shop
Street Address
Town or City
Telephone Number

Work Order Number

Customer Name_____

Address_____

_____

Telephone_____ Postal Code _____

Signature_____

Date
In_____

Date
Promised_____

Description of artwork:

Condition:

Frame Code	Size	United Inches

Liner

Fillet

Glass ☐   Acrylic ☐   None ☐   Other ☐

Type_____

Mats

Top Mat #_____ Colour_____ Top___ Sides_____ Bottom_____

2nd Mat #_____Colour_____ 3/16" ☐ 1/4" ☐ Other_____

3rd Mat #_____Colour_____ 3/16" ☐ 1/4" ☐ Other_____

Vertical

Horizontal

SUB TOTAL $ _____
TAX #1
TAX #2
TOTAL
LESS DEPOSIT
BALANCE

Thank you

I/we have decided not to use conservation
methods in framing this/these items.
Signature_____

How Your Credit Rating Affects Your Business

You may have heard about it, but you may not know how it works. It is your <u>credit rating,</u> and it can make the difference between being granted a loan or turned down for credit, and potentially influence how much interest you will pay. But what exactly is a credit rating?

First, let us dispel a myth. You do not have an overall "rating". Instead, individual financial institutions, credit card issuers, and other creditors assign individual ratings to customers, expressed in a common language. These ratings are kept in a central file by a credit bureau.

Your ratings are reviewed by potential creditors when you apply for credit. These ratings generally indicate whether or not you pay your bills on time. This helps the creditor decide whether or not to proceed with your application.

When you consistently pay according to the terms of your credit, for example, making loan payments on time or paying credit card balances and other bills by the due date, you receive the top consumer rating of 1. If you pay late but within 30-60 days, you will be assigned a rating of 2. Late payments of 60-90 days will reduce your rating to 3.

Serious credit deficiencies can result in much lower ratings. For instance, if you pay off delinquent debts under a consolidation order or similar arrangement, your rating will be a 7. An 8 indicates items paid for on credit have been repossessed and a 9 indicates a write-off, usually a bad debt or referral to a collection agency. Creditors generally supply your local credit bureau with ratings every month. Your files are updated to include current ratings, as well as a historical record for several years.

When you apply for credit, you may be declined by a financial institution if you have a series of unsatisfactory ratings. At the very least, the institution may charge you a higher interest for the risks associated in lending to someone with an unstable repayment history or lower credit rating. The best way to avoid either of these situations is to simply pay your bills on time. But how do you know if the information in your file is accurate?

You can contact your local credit bureau and request the same information that credit grantors consider when assessing your application. The first step is to find your credit bureau. Usually it is listed in the phone book.

Enquire whether you need an appointment to review your file. Some bureaus allow you to walk in and look at your file, while others require advance notice. Make sure you agree with your ratings and any other details in your file. If you discover mistakes, ask the credit bureau staff what action you can take to rectify the situation. If there is a dispute over a rating submitted by a creditor, ask to include a note in your file explaining your side of the story.

If you have never checked your credit bureau file, you will never know whether it is accurate. You should certainly check if you have ever been turned down for credit. Even if you have had no problem, it is a good idea to review your file every year.

CHAPTER FOURTEEN

Glazing

One of the obligations, among several, required of a picture framer is to protect and enhance artwork in a manner that complements the subject matter and yet does not detract from it. An essential aspect of the framing process is the glazing. Glass provides a barrier between the art and the environment in which it is placed, such as pollutants, insects, moisture and handling.

Of course light is essential for viewing art, but the ultraviolet component of most light sources is extremely harmful, permanently, to the artwork. It is therefore essential that this part of the frequency spectrum be blocked, or filtered out before it strikes the art. Ultraviolet radiation causes paper to become brittle with deterioration of colour and loss of brightness. These damages are permanent. A coating of an ultraviolet blocking agent is fused to the glass which filters out the harmful rays, but at the same time, it must not diminish the clarity of the art.

Float glass is one of the processes in the production of glass and the choice for picture framers. It is polished to a constant thickness (or thinness) of from 1mm to 18mm. Picture framing glass is 2mm thick. The combined ingredients of glass are silica sand (about 90 per cent of the bulk), soda ash, dolomite, limestone and a practical amount of cullet (broken or waste glass collected for re-melting). These are combined to form the "batch." Strict quality control and carefully monitored temperature throughout the process are maintained.

The batch materials are fed into a furnace which produces a constant temperature of 1600°C. A continuous ribbon of molten glass floats on a bath of molten tin. Imperfections are melted out, ensuring flat, parallel surfaces.

The glass is then annealed (process of heating and cooled slowly) to strengthen it and cooled to 200°C, relieving stress which prevents splitting and breaking in the cutting phase. The glass ribbon is cut automatically on the move.

Blown glass, rolled glass and pressed glass are processes that have been used to produce flat glass, such as for windows, for over 800 years. But, as stated above, float glass is the type preferred by professional picture framers because of its uniform thickness and superior transparency qualities.

There are four main classifications of glass:

• regular (clear) glass
• non-glare - single-sided and double-sided
• ultraviolet filtering
• anti-reflection; coated and non-coated.

Regular, clear, plain

All glass have the following qualities:

• Normally 2mm to 2.51mm in thickness.
• A high light transmission quality as high as 91 per cent.
• Blocks about 42 per cent of ultraviolet radiation.
• Reflects 8 per cent, a reflection referred to as the "mirror effect" which creates distracting images on the glass from surrounding objects preventing the viewer from seeing the artwork clearly.
• Although it resists scratching and static charges when compared with acrylic glazing, its weight becomes a factor as the size increases.

Non-glare glass

This type of regular glass is etched (pitted) by a chemical process to prohibit light reflection. It has a more translucent rather than transparent quality. The result is perceptible vision distortion when separated from the artwork by more than one or two mat board layers. This classification of glass has the following characteristics:

- It may be single-side or double-side etched.
- Light transmission is 87 per cent compared to 91 per cent for plain glass.
- It reflects about 4 per cent of light, compared to 8 per cent for plain glass.
- Although it is etched with a chemical, usually an acid, the residual acid has been completely purged and so it presents no danger to the artwork.
- Unless otherwise stated by the manufacturer, non-glare glass does not improve ultraviolet blocking over regular glass.
- In the case of single-side etched glass, the etched side faces away from the artwork.

Anti-reflective (reflection free)

This glass tends to be nearly invisible when placed over artwork, that is to say, its light transmission is substantially increased and the reflection is reduced. The process used to achieve this is by either applying a special optical coating to the glass surface or by micro-etching the surface;

- Optical coating process can make the glass expensive.
- It can be reflective when viewed from an angle.
- The coating may de-laminate over time.
- The coating is less flexible than the glass substrate.
- Some cleaners and fingerprints may mark coated glass.
- Micro-etching is achieved by etching the glass twice, creating finer facets on the glass surface.

Ultraviolet filtering (blocking)

This type of glass has been defined as that product which blocks more than 90 per cent of the total UV spectrum, that is, 300 to 400 nanometres, and more than 97 per cent of the UV spectrum between 300 to 380 nanometres (one nanometre is one-billionth of a metre). The process for producing UV protective glass is by applying a filter coat to the surface of the glass or by laminating a UV filter plastic between two 1mm sheets of glass.

Ultraviolet radiation cannot be eliminated entirely from reaching the artwork. UV blocking glass does not completely protect artwork forever; artwork will still fade and deteriorate over time. What the UV blocking glass does do for the art is it delays deterioration.

Glass that blocks up to 99.5 per cent might mean that this is good up to only 380 nanometres, whereas UV damage occurs up to and beyond 400 nanometres, into the top end of the visible light spectrum, which happens to be violet. So, for choosing UV blocking glass check its blocking ability, not only of the UV portion but also of the UV light part of the spectrum that is impeded.

Cleaning Glass

Most picture framers have "preferred" activities in their workshops such as designing the mats, cutting mats, cutting and joining frames, stretching needlework and object framing. People who derive joy from cleaning glass are in the minority. Cleaning glass is tedious work and it is time consuming resulting in labour costs, however, it has to be done. Modern methods of packaging glass, such as having it cleaned at the factory and then interleaf the sheets of glass with paper, makes the glass more costly. This cost is offset by the labour and cleaning materials which would otherwise be necessary. Glass sheets with paper interleaf require but a minimal amount of attention, mainly dusting them and removal of fingerprints. By wearing cotton gloves you can eliminate much of the dust and all of the fingerprints. Having the sheets sprayed with powdered resin (which must be removed before cleaning) is a common alternative to paper, but then the cleaning itself drives up the cost of labour and cleaning materials.

Place the panel of glass on a clean table and remove the powder using a dusting brush. Mist the surface with a commercial cleaner, but one that does not contain ammonia (a strong alkali) or vinegar (acid) or even colouring. This applies particularly for conservation framing where a residual presence of acid or alkali could have a harmful effect on the artwork. One other cleaning agent is isopropyl alcohol, especially suitable for micro-etched glass. In all cases, follow the manufacturer's instructions for cleaning.

Wipe the surface of the glass with industrial paper towels or with lint-free fabric towels, such as flannelette, until dry. By holding the glass over a dark surface, such as a piece of mat board or holding it up to the light, streaks, if present, will show up.

Remember, the glass edges are sharp, so when drying it off be extra careful. It is a good idea to "swipe" the glass with a seamer or carborundum (whet stone) prior to cleaning. It takes only a few seconds but it prevents unnecessary shedding of blood.

Cutting Glass

Although the tool used to "cut" glass is a glass cutter, it does not actually cut glass. It scores the glass. Glass is anomalous; that is, it is in a semi-solid state at temperatures below 540°C. It lacks definite stratification or crystalline structure – Figure A. As a result breaks in glass are inclined to run in erratic configurations. The action of the glass cutter temporarily arranges the glass molecules in a linear arrangement along the scored line – Figure B. Once the cut has been made, the glass must be snapped off immediately otherwise the glass will "heal" and be all but impossible to break – Figure C. It is not the scored line that heals, but rather the molecules rearrange themselves in the previous random fashion.

The illustrations on the next page show the three stages.

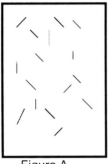
Figure A

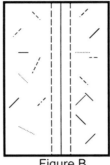
Figure B

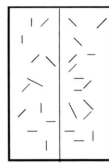
Figure C

Set the cleaned sheet of glass on a hard, clean work surface. The glass cutter usually has a tungsten (brittle, heavy metallic element) wheel, although carbide wheels and diamond tipped cutters are also used. The metallic wheels are tempered and brittle, so care must be taken both when in use and the way they are stored. Dropping the cutter and cutting gritty glass can damage the wheel. Cutters are stored in a container with light oil or kerosene.

To make the cut, hold the cutter firmly and apply just enough pressure to score the glass. Use a straight edge or T-square to keep the cutting "on track." The cutting wheel must be held perpendicular to the glass surface and the cut is made with one swipe, starting about ¼" from the starting, or far edge and continuing to the nearest edge. If the cutter skips for one reason or another, do not attempt to re-cut that side, but rather turn the glass over and cut the other side. Going over a cut score for the second time, or going over skips in the line, ruins the cutter wheel.

Wall-mounted glass-cutting machines usually combine three cutting functions, cutting cardboard, glass and plastic sheeting. There several advantages in using this type of equipment. Consider:

The tension on the cutter wheel can be adjusted for a consistent pressure.

- It is much easier to train people on this machine than doing it by hand.
- There is a potential for less wastage.
- The vertical and horizontal measuring scales eliminate manual measuring and marking.

J. Edwin Warkentin

- Production stops make mass cutting of the same size glass much quicker.
- It is more efficient and so more productive.

If you have a wall-mounted cutter in your shop does not mean that you can discard the hand-held model. You will find it useful when cutting oval, circle and odd shaped patterns.

Cutting an oval piece of glass by hand you:

- Trace out the pattern with a permanent marker pen, around the inside rabbet of the frame.
- Using your cutter, lightly score the glass around the pattern you have drawn.
- Turn the glass over on the table and press the scored line so that it runs all the way around.
- Now score lines 1/8" from the oval to the outside edge of the glass.
- Turn the glass over and press over the lines; the pieces should fall away.
- If small points are left on the oval glass, they can be removed with either glass pliers or one of the notches on the glass cutter.

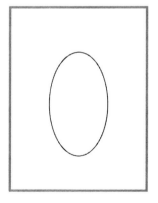

the pattern 'scored' on the glass

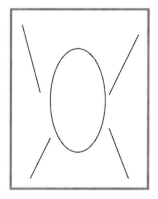

release lines scored 1/8" from the oval

Acrylics

These materials are classified as thermoplastics, a synthetic resinous substance that can be shaped or moulded into any shape, generally referred to simply as plastics. Their introduction to the picture framing industry, first as a liquid used in painting and finishing wood, and then in sheets for glazing, revolutionized both aspects. It is the latter that has had a great impact on picture framing.

Acrylic, in the form of sheets, have recognizable trade names such as Plexiglas, Lucite, Acrylite, Perspex - just to mention a few. Then there are plastic sheets, other than acrylic, such as polycarbonate and polystyrene, made from other chemicals. The latter two have qualities that also make them useful in picture framing. Polycarbonate has a high impact resistance making it virtually unbreakable. Polystyrene is sufficiently strong enough for picture framing but it should not be hung in direct sunlight because it turns yellow or hazy. It is the least expensive of the lot. Acrylic is by far the most popular glazing material, other than glass, in picture framing. It comes in clear, non-glare and UV filtering.

Cutting acrylic is done with either an electric table saw with metal-cutting blades or with an inexpensive hand-held plastic cutter. The wall mounted cutter described above, under "glass" has a blade made for cutting plastic sheets. Whichever cutting method is chosen, remember to leave the cover paper or "cover" on the sheet. This cover protects the fragile surface of the acrylic and should be removed just prior to putting it in the frame. Cutting by hand is limited to a thickness of ¼". Here you go over the score mark until you are about one third of the way through, place it on a flat surface such as a table, and with the scored mark at the edge of the flat surface, snap it off.

Cleaning acrylic presents a bit of a problem. Conventional commercial glass cleaners should be avoided. Some are gritty and can scratch the surface while others, especially those that are alcohol-based or solvent-based, cause a chemical reaction with the chemical content of the acrylic making the surface become hazy. Use warm water with a dishwashing liquid or approved acrylic cleaners with an anti-static component. Excessive rubbing results in a static build-up, which is difficult to neutralize. Some features of acrylic glazing worth considering are:

- It is lightweight; about half the weight of glass.

- It is impact resistant; if broken, it will crack, not shatter like glass.

- It is less scratch resistant than glass.

- It holds a static charge; not suitable for easily crumbled media such as pastel and charcoal art.

- It may be cut with a saw or drilled.

Retailer Relations to Suppliers

To succeed in business you are required to attend to hundreds of things. One thing that is often overlooked, to the detriment of long-term growth and profitability, is the need to establish and maintain good supplier relations.

The chief benefit of good supplier relations is stability, whether times are good or bad. If your attitude and response to suppliers are friendly and sincere, they will have an established interest in your success. Referring to an old saying, "if you prosper they prosper." Furthermore, they will be keen to respond to your technical queries and to assist you at every opportunity. This will create mutual respect and trust resulting in transfer of information and assistance when you need it.

Other benefits accrue from good supplier relations. They produce a business mood calculated to generate lower prices, greater discounts, improved quality and quicker deliveries. Your supplier system is the basis of your business, the better your relations with each of your suppliers, the better your profit margin.

During a decline in economic activity or prosperity, supplier relations are especially important., especially at a time when there is a greater demand on everyone to deliver products and services at minimal cost. During those occasions you have two alternatives to maintain your profit margins: one, requesting support from your suppliers or, two, increasing your prices. Price increases are never popular.

The bases of good supplier relations carry no mystery. They are so obvious that they are easily ignored. Besides dealing politely with your suppliers and leaving it at that, consider the following six rules:

1. Show consideration—each of your suppliers is a business person in his or her own right. Respect them as individuals who, like you, are trying to make a living from a small or medium-sized company.

2. Communicate—if you are unhappy with some of the supplier's performance, say so, but in a constructive way. By the same token, commend the supplier for good work.

3. Find out about the supplier's strengths and weaknesses—you should not assume that every supplier is suited to every occasion

4. Honour payment terms—you will be rewarded with loyalty and friendship. In general terms, a reputation of paying your bills on time, or even ahead of time, ensures a cordial relationship, regardless of problems that might come up.

5. Be flexible—if you are asked to extend a time limit or delivery date, or to adjust a purchase quantity or price, and if you can accommodate these requests, do so. You will gain the supplier's gratitude with an understanding that a favour given is a favour to be received.

6. Make allowances for slip-ups or errors—no one is infallible. Minor mistakes or errors should be ignored. Above all, when discussing the problem, stick to the topic and avoid accusations.

CHAPTER FIFTEEN

Stretching and Framing of Art on Canvas

Before we get into proper stretching and framing techniques let's look at some improper framing procedures. A variety of common framing approaches have harmful effects on canvas supported art.

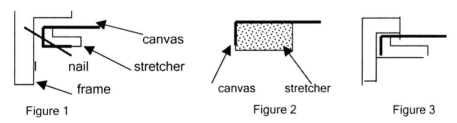

Figure 1   Figure 2   Figure 3

Figure 1, the use of nails to fasten the painting into the frame frequently splits the stretcher frame, punctures the canvas, restricts expansion and contraction and requires powerful hammer blows to the stretcher and frame, resulting in possible damage to part or the whole project.

Figure 2 shows the canvas stretched on a piece of lumber that does not have a raised lip edge. The canvas should have minimal contact with the wood. Wood, because it is acidic, can, over time, severely damage the canvas and the painting. A raised lip is a "must." Some framers actually wrap the stretcher frames, or shrink wrap them in plastic.

Then, in Figure 3 we see an example of the art on canvas being allowed to have its surface touch the lip of the frame resulting in damage, especially if the painting is not completely dry or has been freshly varnished—it will stick to the frame. If this practice is followed and at a later date the canvas art is removed from the frame, tearing of the art will result. Another precaution is to never let the painted surface come in contact with any glazing material.

Framing Methods

Correct framing not only enhances the object being framed but also provides protection. The back is protected from insects, dirt and dust by being covered; the front is protected by being recessed behind the front edge of the frame.

All of these advantages are intensified if the framing is done properly. The following ideas are intended to accomplish these objectives. If you have any doubts as to what is proper and what is dubious, you should seek the opinion of a professional conservator.

Stretching

Artwork on canvas is customarily stretched before framing, either by stapling or tacking it to a stretcher frame. It is important that the canvas is stretched with enough tension and drawn tight so that no sagging or wrinkling occurs.

Stretcher bars, usually made from pine, come in various sizes. Before you assemble the stretcher bars to form the frame, check them for flaws, splitting and warping. For large canvases heavier stretcher bars are used and cross braces may be required to prevent the stretcher frame from bowing or deforming—Figure 6.

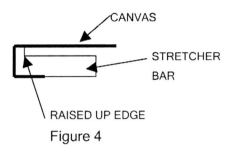

Figure 4

Cross Bracing may be necessary

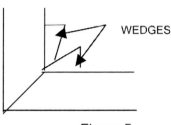

WEDGES

Figure 5

Scrap Mat Board corners may be stapled temporarily to the reverse side of the stretcher frame to keep square prior to fastening the canvas

A stapler with light tension and rustproof staples are used to attach the canvas to the stretcher frame; copper tacks may also be used. The canvas, painted side out, is aligned on the stretcher frame. Staple one side at the centre, then pull the canvas taut either by hand or with canvas stretching pliers and staple the opposite side. Staple the third and the fourth side in similar fashion. A diamond shaped stretch pattern will appear—Figure 8.

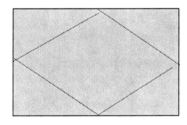

Pattern showing on canvas resulting from eing pulled taut and stapled

Figure 9

Edge view of the canvas on the stretcher frame with the staples at 45° to even out the stress on the canvas threads

Figure 8

Keep on pulling and applying tension from the centre out to the corners. Place a staple on each side of the centre staple on the stretcher bar where you started and proceed to the opposite side and so on, spaced at regular intervals. Staples should be placed at 45° angles to even out the stress on the canvas threads—Figure 9. Having done this all around the stretcher frame will give an even wrinkle-free job and the diamond shaped pattern will have disappeared.

A Monroe, or tucked corner—Figure 10, is used to finish the corners. Excess canvas should not be cut off. It should be extended over the back of the stretcher frame and held in place with a few staples.

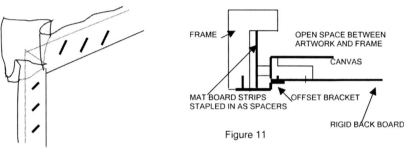

FRAME
OPEN SPACE BETWEEN ARTWORK AND FRAME
CANVAS
MAT BOARD STRIPS STAPLED IN AS SPACERS
OFFSET BRACKET
RIGID BACK BOARD

Figure 11

CORNERS ARE FINISHED IN SUCH A MANNER AS TO ALLOW THE STRETCHER BARS TO BE EXPANDED WITHOUT STRAINING THE CANVAS AT THE CORNER, AND STILL BE NEAT

Figure 10

The temporary corner pieces—Figure 7, should be removed at this time and a rigid board attached with screws to facilitate easy removal. The rigid board has several purposes:

- it keeps the stretcher frame square.
- it prevents the reverse side of the canvas from being dented or pierced.
- it also keeps out dust and insects.

Ventilation holes in the rigid board may be covered with a screen. It is important to keep the artwork away from the lip of the frame. To achieve this you might use strips of 4-ply mat board stapled into the edge of the stretcher frame and fitted so the artwork is isolated from the frame—Figure 11.

CHAPTER SIXTEEN

Laminating

If you have a dry mount press or a heated vacuum press for mounting prints and posters, the next natural progression for you is to get into the laminating business. Laminating posters, prints and photographs will provide your customers an alternative to glass, a lightweight, unbreakable, washable material, resistant to handling hazards, with considerable ultra-violet filtering ability and permanent. For you, it will result in additional profits.

Laminates are films of plastic permanently applied to a great variety of art, maps, blue prints, prints and even three dimensional objects such as dried flowers and leaves to seal them and provide permanent protection. Laminating films come in various widths and finishes from glossy, semi-gloss, and patterned like linen weave. A foam blanket is placed on top of the "sandwich" to allow air and moisture to escape. The film should be perforated prior to application to ensure a proper bond.

The project, prior to insertion in the heat press, should have the following components arranged from the bottom up:

- A sheet of release paper,
- Artwork bonded to a substrate (mounting board),
- Laminating film,
- Foam overlay
- Finally, another sheet of release paper.

The heat press temperature varies from 85°C to 105°C and the time for the process to complete varies from 5 to 15 minutes depending on the type of laminating film and press used.

It is important to understand the difference between laminating and encapsulation. Laminating emphasizes that the item will be sealed permanently, non-reversible, under a plastic film. In some cases the film is applied to both sides of the object. Encapsulation is a method, free from impurities, used to preserve and protect documents from harmful contaminants. The process requires two sheets of 3 to 5mm acid-free polyester film joined with double-sided tape and the item in between the sheets. As with other conservation methods, encapsulation is totally reversible.

Most picture framers and photographers are well-acquainted with dry mounting but there are many who do not know the great profit possibility of laminating. The procedure is easy and inexpensive. It requires a heat press and a bit of experimenting. The many ways to ingeniously enhance and significantly enrich the value of your prints and posters will become clear very quickly. By considering and trying out the following exercises you will develop your own artistic results and soon find out just how easy laminating actually is.

Custom Mats

A delightful way to highlight a mat, print or photograph is to laminate clusters of pressed dried flowers, leaves, fronds or ribbons onto a mat corner.

1. Choose your design and its location on the mat board.

2. To hold the items solidly in place, apply a small quantity of glue behind each item and place it into position; let the glue set before proceeding.

3. Select the pre-perforated laminating film (finish suitable for the project), cut an oversize piece of film and place it over the layout being careful to place it correctly the first time since it is impossible to reposition the film without disturbing the objects.

4. Cover with the foam overlay blanket and place on a sheet of release paper larger than the laminating film, then into the heat press,

under pressure, for two or three minutes.

5. Remove and trim the excess film.

6. Should any air pockets be present around the items, make a hole in the film, replace the foam blanket and return it into the heat press for an additional minute.

Note: Confetti or sand may be used to accentuate the mat; in these cases cover the area lightly with glue and sprinkle the confetti or sand over this area and allow it to dry.

Texturing the Mat

Laminating film in combination with materials such as canvas, grass cloth, course sacking, fine wire mesh or other embossing matter, applied to the mat provides selections of surfaces that differ from the ordinary.

1. Place a sheet of laminating film over the mat board and cover it with whatever embossing surface you have selected. Then cover the entire project with a foam blanket.

2. Place in the heat press for about one minute.

3. After removal and inspection, if satisfied with the results, cut the mat in the usual way.

Try experimenting with crinkled aluminum foil, crumpled release paper or glazing foil, by placing it on top of the laminated mat, cover with a foam blanket and insert in the heat press. The result is a unique pattern embossed into the film and also into the mat.

Image Transfer to Canvas

Another impressive use of the heat press is the transferring of photographs and prints to canvas, simulating oil or acrylic paintings. The canvas is then stretched onto stretcher bars and framed.

There are several ways of accomplishing the transfer of images to canvas; some use a waterproof emulsion which is time consuming and expensive. By far the quickest and equally efficient system is to use laminating film. Even so, it is advisable to experiment on prints or photographs of little value. As in most activities, practice is the maxim.

1. Decide on the laminating film to be used. Generally for this purpose a semi-gloss finish is used, although glossy type is preferred by some customers. Cut a piece 2½" larger on each side than the article to be treated.

2. Lightly run a perforator over the top side of the film (assuming that the laminate is not pre-perforated) before it is placed over the item to be treated. The perforations should be about ¼" apart.

3. Carefully remove the release paper from the film a little bit at a time and apply the film to the item. Smooth it out with a soft cloth ensuring that air pockets are removed.

4. With release paper under it and a foam blanket on top place the combination into the press and leave it there for five minutes at 85°C.

5. Remove the project from the press.

6. If the subject is a photograph, and before it has cooled off, lift the paper backing off. If this method fails, and it might, especially in the case of large photographs, immerse the item in a tray of water for about half an hour. Then peel off the backing paper; a scouring pad may be used in this process. This method is recommended for prints and posters as the backing papers on these forms of art are relatively thin and hard to remove using the dry method.

7. Cut a piece of mounting film slightly smaller than the laminating film and place it on the back of the project. Flatten it from the centre outwards to drive out all the air.

8. Choose a piece of canvas approximately 3" wider, on each side, than the image.

9. Place the combination in the centre of the canvas ensuring that the weave of the canvas is straight in relation to the picture.

10. Place the combination, covered with a foam blanket, into the heat press for four minutes at 85°C.

11. Remove the item from the press and you have your print transferred to canvas. Now it just remains to be stretched onto stretcher bars and framed.

J. Edwin Warkentin

Place-Mats and Similar Items

Although this section has scarcely an association with picture framing, it is an extension for the use of laminating and the heat press. Place-mats, menus, coasters and other unusual items can be mounted and laminated onto a rigid board to present a very attractive gift idea for the impulse buyer and also for the thrifty shopper. These items, although intended primarily for the domestic market, have their place in the commercial trade as well.

Consider setting aside a space in your gallery with a plain table setting which would include some of these products. The visible display will do the marketing for you. Things for processing, other than menus, might include old maps, photographs of a personal or general nature, floral designs or prints suited to the locale. A suggested procedure follows:

1. Cut the hardboard (for example, Masonite®) to the size of the image.

2. Make sure that the edges are smooth and the corners are rounded. A sanding block may be used for this.

3. Mount the print to the hardboard using mounting film and the heat press.

4. Cover the project with laminating film—a textured surface might be preferred since it resists scuffs.

5. Cover it with the foam blanket and place in the heat press.

6. Upon examination, once it is removed from the press, if the surface is not acceptable, return it to the press for another couple of minutes.

7. Trim off the excess film and put tape around the surface perimeter.

8. Again, sand the edges with fine sandpaper then paint the edges with a matching colour using a felt marker or paint; remove the tape by pulling it toward the outside edge rather than towards the middle in order to prevent lifting the print.

9. Cover the back with soft cloth or felt and there you have it.

Wood Mounting for Certificates, Newspaper Articles

A wall plaque portraying a certificate or some other testimonial of a personal nature such as one that might be highlighted in a newspaper account is often not visualized by potential customers in a framing gallery. A wall plaque portraying a document is a lasting tribute for the individual. It might be a letter of recognition from a government agency, the local chamber of commerce or a calling to mind of a long service award. Local school boards, service clubs, business groups and similar agencies, are possibilities for presentation plaques for their associates. Here is how this is done using ½" medium density particle board (MDF); plywood may also be used:

1. Cut a board to the size of the certificate, letter or. . .

2. Sand the edges to a smooth, even finish.

3. With mounting tissue and the heat press mount the item to the wood base.

4. Cover the project with a laminating film and the foam blanket then insert into the heat press; leave it there for approximately three minutes.

5. Remove from the press and trim the excess film.

6. Tape the surface perimeter, preferably with removable tape, and sand the edges once more with fine sandpaper; be careful to not sand against the top surface to avoid lifting the laminated article.

7. Paint the edges with a suitable colour (it can be water-based paint), let it dry then carefully remove the tape.

8. If you have a router, carve a slot at the back, near the top for hanging.

CHAPTER SEVENTEEN

Needlework

Today's picture framing industry has become big business. Growth is evident in the framing of oils, water-colours, limited edition prints and original graphics. More people can now discuss, with awareness, processes such as serigraphs, lithographs and limited edition prints. However, nowhere has the interest been as dramatic as in the popularity of needle art.

Every year, needlework framing is attracting a larger share of the total picture framing business. Many framers specialize in framing needlework and some have made it their sole activity.

With so many framers now handling needlework, numerous techniques regarding stretching and framing are being tried; some are good, some are average while still others cause severe damage to fine needle art. So this subject matter offers both opportunity and peril. Done properly with conservation in mind, needlework framing means great satisfaction, large sales and good profits. Done poorly or indifferently result in substantial losses for the customer and the framer.

Most picture framers who handle needlework enjoy it. The blocking and stretching can be challenging, tedious and at times frustrating but the total job from designing the layout to customer pick up is immensely rewarding.

What is Needlework?

When customers bring their needlework projects to you for framing they may be nervous or apprehensive. Many hours of labour, sometimes as many as hundreds, lies on your sales table. You need to be professional enough to recognize and appreciate the needlework. Recognizing the type of needlework is often enough to relieve the customer's initial anxiety.

The reason for learning about the different kinds of needlework is to develop competency for framing them. By knowing more about how the pieces are made you can do a better inspection job when you take the order, such as being aware of missing stitches, narrow borders and soiled areas. Some of the different types of needle art are listed below.

Crewel – the yarn used for this type of tapestry or embroidery work is a thin, lightly twisted two-ply worsted yarn. Traditionally, crewel was referred to as "crewel embroidery" since it uses many of the embroidery stitches and is usually done on tightly woven linen or cotton fabric—sometimes on wool. The stitches are long and the general fine feel of embroidery is gone, giving way to bolder colours and designs. Needlework shops often sell crewel kits with the images stamped onto the fabric. Crewel works are rarely matted or placed under glass.

Crochet – from the French *croche*—hook. Crochet work is done with a needle having a hook on one end. Threads, such as crochet cotton or other yarns are interwoven and knotted to form an open weave or lace pattern. Heavier yarns can be crocheted into clothing such as sweaters.

Bargello – this is a type of needlework done on needlepoint canvas. Straight up and down stitches are made skipping as many holes as needed to affect the pattern. Bargello, since the requirement is to not thread each hole in the canvas, is quick since it covers a lot of canvas and colourful patterns are easily done.

Cross-stitch – or, frequently referred to as 'counted cross-stitch', is in the embroidery class of needlework. This popular needlework is done stitching small X's on to either linen or cotton cloths, having an even weave. The X's form the pattern of the design. The thread used is generally cotton or embroidery floss. The strands of thread are, at times, separated to affect smaller stitches. Although stamped designs on the cloth support may be purchased, generally, the pattern design is determined by counting the X's required to complete the motif.

Needlepoint – is characterized by the type of supporting material it is worked on—canvas. This canvas, again, is different from artists' canvas, in that it is really a tough, open mesh grid. Needlepoint is a type of embroidery on the canvas described, covering it completely with coloured yarn. The size of the image particulars determines the size of the canvas grids— varying from 4 to 24 (the number of  mesh squares per inch), and the size of the fibre used to create the pattern.

Just a word about the canvases used in needlework, besides the mesh sizes, there are two grid structures that should be noted. MONO canvas has single one strand threads forming a horizontal and vertical matrix. PENELOPE grids are formed by placing paired threads in the horizontal and vertical dimensions close together; see illustrations below.

MONO   PENELOPE

Petit Point – is a variety of needle art done on a fine mesh canvas— typically from 20 to 40 mesh squares per inch, using a fine needle and, whereas needlepoint typically uses three-strand yarn, petit point uses one- or two-strand cotton or silk yarn for this extremely fine work. Also, whereas needlepoint covers the entire canvas with stitches, petit point is concerned only with the image, leaving the background exposed. Petit point is often included with regular needlepoint done on penelope canvas to fill in facial features and other fine details.

Batik – from the Javanese word meaning *painted*, is a method of dyeing textiles by applying wax to parts to be left uncoloured. Wax is applied to those areas of the fabric, usually cotton but other fabrics such as silk and fine linen, that are to retain the white or off-white natural colour. Then the cloth is dipped into the lightest colour of the project. This part is then waxed to the shape of its design. The fabric is inserted into the next brightest colour. This process is repeated until the design pattern is complete, at which time the fabric is immersed into boiling water to remove the wax.

Mola – is a form of reverse appliqué developed by the Cuna Indians of Central America. It involves sewing coloured layers of cloth on top of each other with each succeeding layer smaller than the previous one, but forming a designed pattern, until the last layer is exposed in its entirety. A portion of each layer is revealed and with embroidery added, this form of art has widespread appeal. Molas may be stretched first of all by stitching it onto fabric which is already stretched on stretcher frames so the whole of the piece is visible, then framed behind glass but spaced away from it.

Needlework – bits and pieces

Blocking

Only needlework badly off square should be blocked before it is stretched. Most puckering can be pulled out during the stretching process. If you do decide to block the piece make sure that the yarns are colourfast before applying moisture to relax the threads.

A blocking board can be made from a rigid piece of plywood or any such material that will take tacks and staples. The board should be covered with a heavy, clean white fabric marked off in one inch squares, using a permanent pen.

The needlework may be rolled up in a damp towel for several hours, or a steam iron may be used to soften the threads. Stretch it on the blocking board. Starting at the middle of each side pin the item into place, then continue toward the corners on each side. Staples may be used if the supporting material is of a canvas type material.

Stretching Bases

Although there are many techniques used by framers for stretching needlework, some must be avoided for the preservation of the needlework and the protection of the framer. Stretching supports include the following—each having its characteristics:

8-ply rag board — the highest quality mounting board for all needlework.

- Foam centre board (acid free)—very good for "pinning."
- Mounting board—should be shrink- wrapped or otherwise covered to keep it isolated from the needlework; accepts staples.
- Wooden stretcher bars—should be sealed before attaching fabric.
- Upson™ board—not recommended; it deteriorates readily.
- Masonite™—not recommended due to lignin present and the presence of oils in the case of tempered Masonite,.

Mounting Methods

There are probably as many mounting methods for needlework, or variations thereof, as there are framers framing needlework. In this section we will discuss the mounting procedures that will protect and preserve the item to be framed. Among these are lacing, pinning and stapling; the latter would not be applicable for all types of needlework.

Lacing – is the preferred method of mounting needlework for conservation purposes since it leaves the mounted fabric art in its original condition. There is very little risk of damage when using this technique for mounting needlework. This is also the approved way for mounted needlework as required by many guilds for juried competition purposes.

The major drawback in lacing is that it is time consuming and therefore framers must of necessity charge more. Only about five per cent of needlework framers lace their projects on a regular basis. Another nuisance is that lacing is difficult to do if the assignment is out-of-square.

Lacing provides a constant tension to keep the stitches uniformly in place. It involves no element that might be harmful to the needlework or its fabric base, such as tapes, glue or staples.

The lacing material itself should be of a good quality yarn, preferably of the same material and weight as that of the fabric being worked on. Cotton yarn of the same weight as the material being laced will, in most cases, satisfy the lacing component. The needle used should not be so large as to push the fibres apart too much. A small size darning needle or a tapestry needle will do the job. It might be worthwhile to tape the raw fabric edges with acid-free tape to prevent them from fraying out.

The mounting or support board must be of 8-ply rag board or acid-free foam centre board. Cut the board to size using a straight, rather than a bevel, cut. Sand the edges lightly to get rid of the sharp edges which could damage the fabric being stretched. Place the needlework over the support board, positioning it where it is intended to end up. Insert map tacks (this type is short, has a large head and is sharply pointed—other pins will do) at the corners to hold the piece into place. These pins will be removed after the lacing is completed.

Start by joining the opposite corners as in Fig. A. Then lace the long dimension of the project as in Fig. B. Ensure that you have a long enough thread to complete the side. When you have completed the long side lacing, with stitches no more than ½" apart, tie it off and start working the stitches back to the starting point in order to achieve tension. After this step is completed, tie that end off too. Then do the same procedure with the other two sides, Fig. C. While these steps are being taken, make sure that the needlework is straight and parallel. The needle art is now ready for framing, Fig. D, with or without mats. If glass is to be included, enough mat boards or spacers must be included to prevent the glass from touching the needlework.

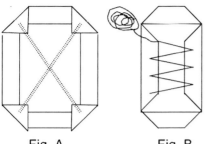
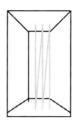
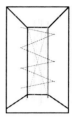

| Fig. A | Fig. B | Fig. C | Fig. D |

Pinning – Since the demand for having needlework laced is rather small, picture framers have found other ways of stretching and mounting fabric art. Pinning is such an alternative. It is worth repeating that mounting and framing of needlework is of conservation quality if it is 100 per cent reversible to its original state.

Pinning is done on an acid-free foam centre board. These boards come in various thickness from 1/8" to 1/2"; the thicker, of course, the stronger it is. For light weight needlework, 1/8" to 3/16" is suitable.

Cut the foam board to size, once you have determined how much of the image will be visible. If padding is to be used, cut it to the same size. Find the centre points on each side and insert a pin at that point, at the same time stretching the fabric. For pinning, stainless steel straight pins are used. If the canvas is of the mesh type, such as mono or penelope, use 1/2" stainless steel nails—with large, flat heads.

Working from the centre pins, place pins every 1/2" towards each corner. Periodically check to make sure that the weave of the fabric is perfectly straight. In fact, you might want to leave the pins not pushed in entirely so that you can correct any misalignment once the entire project is finished. Then push the pins in all the way. Fasten the loose ends at the back with one or two pins at each corner.

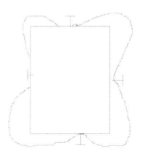
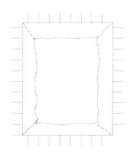

Stapling – Stapling is the run-of-the-mill mounting method carried out by some picture framers of needlework; It is quick and economical. There are several dangers associated with stapling. Among them are: staples rusting unless stainless steel staples are used, and tearing the fabric.

There are two methods of securing the needlework to the mounting board with staples—A. from the back and B. from the front.

If A is selected, cut a mounting board from 8-ply rag board to the size required. If padding is required, cut it to the same size. Centre the needlework on the front of the board, pinning the corners temporarily. Turn the project over and place a staple at the middle of each side. Proceed to staple from the middle of each side to the corners. Check the pattern regularly to make sure it is coming out the way it should. Then fold the excess fabric neatly at the back and staple it into place.

If B is selected and a mat must be included to cover the staples, if stapled from the front of the item, cut a mounting board large enough to accommodate the image and provide support for the mat.

Once the fabric is in place, put a staple in the middle of each side to hold it in place. Then proceed to staple toward the corners. An office stapler with rust free staples is adequate to do the job.

The Foam Core Board Process – is a method which can be applied with laced or pinned mounting methods. Method 1 or Method 2, can be undertaken without previous mountings.

Method 1. Prior to lacing or pinning, cut a piece of foam core board to the outside dimensions, including the mat. Once this is done, cut the centre of the foam board to the dimensions of the needlework to be visible once it is framed. Then cut 1/8" off two adjacent sides of this board to accommodate the stretched needlework. When the needlework is stretched, replace the unit into the opening created. Cut the mat board borders to size and continue with the balance of the framing procedure.

Method 2. Place the needlework over the opening in the foam board; make sure that the image is centred and the lines are straight. Prepare the foam board as in Case 1 but do not trim off the 1/8" bits. Press the foam board "fall-out" back into place. From the back, stretch the fabric into position; the close fit will hold the piece in place. Cut the mat board opening a bit smaller than the foam board opening to cover the edges of the stretched needlework.

More things to consider:

- If you are framing a Chinese silk embroidery, you might want to sew it onto a thinly padded mounting board with a sewing machine; the padding will eliminate wrinkling often present in the background fabric near the embroidery.

- Tapes, glues and adhesive-coated boards present a difficult time for reversing mounted processes; they can stain and in some cases cause irreparable damage.

- If the needlework is too small to fold over the mounting board for stretching, sew pieces of cotton or linen to the edges.

- Polyester, available at fabric shops, is the preferred material for padding needlework; it will not mildew, discolour, stain, break down or become matted; it will not harm the needlework.

- If you are uncertain regarding the pH quality of mounting boards, and this applies especially to stretcher bars, either cover them with cotton fabric or better still, shrink-wrap them.

- Avoid putting glass right up to the needlework; if the customer wants glass but no mat, place spacers under the frame rabbet.

- If you are tempted to add needlework supplies to your stock, be careful; stocking these supplies permits you to diversify your product assortment; it will bring in new customers for these products and potential framing sales; however (there usually is a 'however'), do you really understand and value needlework? Can you afford the inventory necessary to satisfy the serious needlework customers and do you have the space and the time to take care of this new venture?

- You should never assume responsibility that the threads in the needlework are permanently colour-fast; if moisture, whether by steam iron or damp towel, must be used prior to blocking, it is wise to take a snip off each coloured thread from the back of the needlework and test it with water for colour stability.

- The majority of experienced framers are convinced that protective sprays should be avoided for needlework, particularly since the long-term effects are unknown; what is known is that protective sprays seal the fibres, thereby preventing the needlework from "breathing", and sprays also tend to dull the colours of the needlework.

- Inspect the needlework for any missed stitches; it is best to identify any missed stitches prior to stretching the needlework.

- Soiled needlework, in most cases, must be cleaned; the exception is where the customer refuses to have it cleaned and where the mat will cover the unclean parts—usually in the supporting canvas nevertheless, you are advised to not try cleaning it yourself unless you are pretty sure of the outcome.

CHAPTER EIGHTEEN

Glass Etching

This section will give you all the basic techniques necessary for surface etching. By reading and following them closely you will, right from the beginning, build into your work correct habits which will lead to consistent professional results.

Step 1. Be careful when choosing and preparing the design. If it is a commercial design, follow the directions of application, if it is your design make certain that the cut edges are clean.

Step 2. The choice and preparation of glass also deserves careful attention. Clear glass with no film or smudges is essential.

Step 3. The actual etching will take less time than the first two steps but its success is very dependent on how well the first two steps were done.

Etching is a beautiful way to decorate the surface of a piece of glass. It is elegant and expressive in a way that is far out of proportion to the ease of producing it. In other words, it is much easier to do than you would suspect by looking at the finished product. The basic form of etching is called surface etching.

There has been an incredible surge of interest in etched glass in recent years, both from consumers and artists. Potential buyers have discovered that etched glass is a lovely form of art on its own as well as an enhancement to the framing of paper-borne art.

Glass etching is the abrading or roughening of the surface of a piece of glass in selected areas in order to produce a desired design. There are two general types of glass etching: **sandblasting** (more often done with aluminum oxide rather than sand), and **hydrofluoric acid.** A type of very light etching can be produced with different types of etching creams which contain a "softer" form of this acid and which is safer to use than the undiluted acid, if the directions are carefully followed.

Project:

1. Select a piece of glass 8" X 10"; clean it thoroughly.

2. Attach contact paper to one side.

3. Draw a design similar to that shown.

4. With a sharp knife cut the design; lift the fragments from the glass. Clean the exposed glass thoroughly.

5. Apply etching cream and let it stand for approximately fifteen minutes.

6. Thoroughly wash cream from the glass with running water, making sure that none of the etching cream touches the glass as it is being washed; dry the glass.

7. Remove the remaining contact paper.

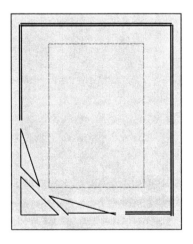

The Baguette

Did anyone think that the early picture framers in Europe were without a sense of humour? The term "baguette", a long strip of wood, comes from the French word for a "long thin loaf" of bread. In practical terms the baguette is an alternative to framing canvases. The strips of wood ¼" to ½" in thickness and from 1¼" to 2" in width, painted, stained or gilded are just that—strips of wood without the standard rabbet found in picture moulding. They may be cut and joined similarly to that of a conventional frame, but they are more likely to be nailed to the stretcher frame, one piece at a time with the corners butted rather than mitred.

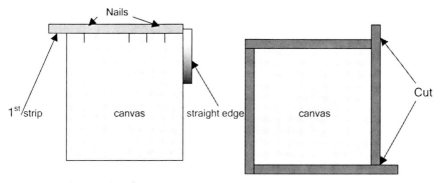

Fig. 1 shows the first strip in place.

Fig. 2 shows all strips in place indicating two of the four extended pieces cut off.

Needed are four strips each about 2" longer than the side to which it will be attached. Place the strips on a flat, solid surface and start the brads in each one, spacing them about 5" apart. Position the brads in the centre of the strips, just in far enough to hold them in place.

Standing the stretcher bar frame with the canvas toward you, place the straight edge along the top of the vertical side so that it extends beyond the horizontal plane of the canvas. Lay a baguette on the top, tight against the straight edge. The face of this strip, and the others too, for that matter, should protrude beyond the face of the canvas far enough to leave the canvas set back 1/8" to ¼." While holding the baguette tightly, remove the straight edge and hammer brads into the stretcher frame. Turn the canvas 90° so that the first side now becomes the "straight edge." The third and fourth side are fastened in the same way. Then, using thin brads, two per corner should be sufficient, reinforce each corner. Finally, saw off the excess pieces of baguette, sand the corners and touch them up.

Preservation of Antique Paper Art

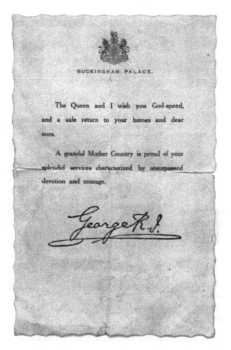

Message from King George V to Canadian troops after World War 1 – 1918

Old water-colour paintings, documents, printed or hand-coloured maps or for that matter any other types of paper-borne art are best displayed framed under glass but without a mat—in other words, they are "floated." To do this, you must be sure that the frame is deep enough to allow for an air space between the glass and the artwork. Antique characteristics of the paper are attractive in themselves, and add to the appeal of the item. The edges of old documents and prints, whether they are ragged or well-preserved, add a degree of authenticity and charm.

Antique prints or documents that have been stored unframed often have finger prints or other soiled areas which need to be cleaned up. To do this, soft erasers rather than liquids of any type are recommended. Thin or delicate paper should be treated with great care, particularly in those sections that have been creased and have loose fibres that could be torn away. Of course, old pencil sketches and faded water-colour paintings must be treated with extra care to avoid further damage to the art.

Many old documents, maps and prints have lain folded or rolled up for many years. They need to be flattened out. It is best to flatten the art first and then to proceed with repairs, assuming repairs are needed. In any case, the art must be flattened before it is framed in an acceptable manner.

The simplest and most direct method to flatten the paper is to moisten the back (mist it, do not soak it) with distilled water. Distilled water ensures that no mineral salts or other foreign ingredients are introduced. Put white blotting paper sheets on both sides of the art, place this under a sheet of glass and add weights and leave to dry. Always test the artwork first to ensure that the colours and inks are permanent. Certain water-colours and inks run when dampened, in which case the "ironing" method is recommended.

The simple method described above may not be the answer for badly damaged or creased paper. A warm pressing iron is often satisfactory to flatten localized wrinkled areas. A severe wrinkle should be dampened slightly and white blotting paper put between the pressing iron and the artwork. Do not use hard pressure nor leave the iron in one place too long —there is the danger of scorching the paper.

Heavy, tough paper may be flattened by putting it under tension. The moistened (again, with a distilled water mist) paper is secured to a firm support, such as a table top, with masking tape (so, masking tape does have a place in the frame shop after all!) on all four sides. One side is taped. The dampened paper is lightly stretched by hand to the opposite side, which is then taped down. The other two sides are dealt with in a similar fashion. As the paper dries it will tighten up and smooth out. Delicate or brittle paper would, no doubt, split if it was treated this way.

To mend a small tear in the artwork, lay it face down on a piece of release paper on a flat surface. Tear, not cut, a piece of mulberry paper large enough to cover the rip. Using wheat or rice starch paste, apply a thin film to the mulberry paper patch. Place the patch over the tear, then release paper and a piece of glass weighted down. Let this dry. Wax paper may be used in place of release paper.

In the case where there is a hole or where the edges of the tear are too far apart to affect a satisfactory mend, one way is to do a "shred-and-paste" patch. The hole (or tear) is patched in the manner described. The "mending" paper, as near as possible to the artwork in texture and colour is shredded to a fine powder consistency and mixed with wheat or rice starch paste. This is then covered with release paper, glass, weights, and let dry.

Old Photographs Never Die They Just Fade Away

(If they are not cared for)

We all know what Queen Victoria looked like. We also know what Sir John A. Macdonald Canada's first prime minister looked like. I know what my great-grandparents looked like when they immigrated to Canada in mid-nineteenth century. We are indeed indebted to the genius who invented and developed the camera.

We assume that images of earlier ancestors or historical characters accurately depict the individual's appearance but we have to depend on the artist's skills and techniques to convey the image to us.

Starting over a hundred and fifty years ago the use of the camera has recorded countless number of people, places and happenings. Along with our families, we have often looked at old photographs of our grandparents and other relatives we have never seen in real life. The camera from its initial style to today's digital equipment rates high on the ranking scale of most significant inventions.

Government buildings have portraits of past executive dignitaries adorning the walls of hallways and offices. Most of the figures are done in oil. Some are even recognizable. Present and past governments have thought it important to preserve these personalities in the eyes and minds of current legislators and the visiting public.

It is equally important to keep likenesses of our grandparents and others before us as reminders of their pioneering spirit, perhaps even as a motivation to carry on where they left off.

Among the important services custom framers dispense is information. If your customers understand why you do the things you are doing, resulting in the preservation of their art, they tend to become steady customers. Keep in mind that when framing photographs you as the framer have the same responsibility to inform your customer as if it were a piece of fine art. It is important to tell the customer what could happen to the photograph if it is placed in a location that will accelerate its destruction.

Photographs are very susceptible to damage caused by light. Photographs placed directly against glass are in danger of sticking to the glass if condensation forms behind the glass or if they are hung in a high humidity area. Great fluctuations of temperature are also harmful. Customers should be encouraged to hang their photographs and fine art where these destructive factors are minimal.

Photographs have played a major part in documenting all sorts of important events. Your duty as a framer is to help safeguard that history as much as possible and still provide a pleasing presentation.

Glass Mat

The art of painting and leafing on glass originated in ancient Rome about 2,000 years ago. At the start, artists painted the back of glass and then scratched out works of art in the dried paint.

As with many other areas of framing, new products have revolutionized old-world methods. Glass matting is one such skill which has become more accessible and practical to the contemporary picture framer. The glass mat is so attractive and unusual that mastering its skill gives a framer an enormous competitive edge.

There are several styles for glass mats, and the technique can really take any direction you choose. The traditional glass mat is black with a leafed panel. Glass mats can be any colour desired with or without a leafed panel. Although there are several methods to make a glass mat, the one described here is perhaps the easiest and yet it has significant appeal.

Project

1. Cover the glass, in our case a piece 8"x 10", with adhesive contact or shelving paper. Burnish it down with a hard plastic squeegee; the adhesive paper serves as a mask.

2. It is carefully scored around the window and the panel to be gilded.

3. Remove the adhesive paper from the outer edge of the mat and between the panel and the window; the window and the panel for gilding are left covered; clean the exposed areas.

4. The glass is then given a solid coat of black paint; two applications are usually sufficient.

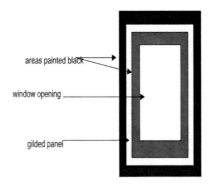

areas painted black
window opening
gilded panel

5. Once the paint has dried, the adhesive film in the area to be gilded is removed.

6. Cut the composition leaf into strips with a razor blade. Apply sizing to the area to be gilded.

7. Lay these strips, one at a time, on a piece of mat board with one end of the leaf hanging over slightly and lower it onto the sized panel until the entire area is covered; smooth it out.

8. Give the gilded area a coat of sizing.

9 .Remove the adhesive film from the window opening.

Giclée Printmaking

The creativity of fine art reproduction has in the last decade become increasingly more exact with the arrival of the dynamic giclée printing process. Giclée, pronounced "zhee-klay", comes from the French verb "gicler" for *spraying of ink;* in fact the process sprays more than four million droplets per second onto acid-free, 100% light fast archival quality paper. In recent years the giclée process has also been applied to reproductions on canvas. The images are first of all scanned and digitally stored in a computer. They are then sent straight away to a high resolution inkjet printer.

The giclée technique of art printing starts with the data entry phase. In other words a scan, that requires the most sophisticated scanning equipment, of an original artwork will produce a digital file which in turn is entered into the associated computer. The operator then harmonizes the file to correspond to the original artwork. The file development can take up to a month for production. Each giclée takes approximately an hour to print.

Giclées are superior to traditional lithography in a number of ways. The colours are brighter and last longer. The range of colours for giclées is far beyond that of lithography. Lithography uses tiny dots of four colours—cyan, magenta, yellow and black. Colours are produced by printing different size dots of these four colours.

Giclées use inkjet technology, superior to the desktop printer. The process employs six colour—light cyan, cyan, light magenta, magenta, yellow and black, of light-fast inks and finer replaceable print heads.

Limited edition litho prints are usually produced in editions of 500 to 1,000, or more but giclée s hardly ever exceed 50 to 100 reproductions First-rate printers vary in price from less than $400.00 to something in the six figure range. The quality of inks used in the process have attained archival degree with over three million colours achievable of highly saturated, non-toxic, water-based ink. The prints produced by the giclée process have a superior resolution to lithographs and the effective colour range exceeds that of serigraphs.

Characteristics in digital inkjet printing are economy and colour quality. The chief concerns regarding the features of this printing process are: the make-up of the substrate, paper or canvas; the quality of the inks; the intensity and radiance of colour replication. No two reproductions are precisely identical. There are delicate, light differences which add to their distinctive quality. Besides offering superior colour reproduction, giclées provide the prospect of an infinite stock of prints, since once the print is digitized, or scanned into the computer, the matter of reproducing is limitless. The quantity printed is up to the artist and the publisher. So in cases where limited editions are planned much of the strategy rests with the integrity of these two participants.

In the past decade much progress has been made with regard to the stability and vibrant colours of inks. Paper and canvas substrates have also been perfected to archival standards. High quality limited edition giclée prints will continue to be produced and their presence in the market-place will only increase.

Glass Trap

Occasionally customers will bring in an old script, restaurant menu, theatre program, letters, statistic records, post cards, and pieces of music or other interesting documents. Most of these attractive pieces have writing or other valuable information on the reverse side which also wants to be seen.

There are two ways in which this can be achieved. One is to encapsulate the item between two pieces of glass, referred to as a Glass Trap, so that it can be viewed from either side. The item is held in place by very small pieces of double-sided tape attached to the glass. The glass is larger than the item to be framed. The glass extending past the art gives the impression of a mat since the space between the art and the frame is transparent, letting the viewer see the background which then "becomes" the mat. The frame is cut and joined in the conventional way, although a groove, the width of the assembled project, can be worked into a piece of moulding lumber and the project set in the groove.

Another, and perhaps the preferred way, is to mat the item on both sides. The two pieces of glass, which are cut to the same outside dimensions as the mats, are placed on each mat and then framed. The mats do not necessarily have to have the same size window openings. In fact, if one image is smaller than the other you might want to make the openings fit the image. One precaution however, if the paper is translucent a problem might arise in that the wider border on one side might be noticeable from the other side through the paper being framed.

The frame used must have sufficient rabbet depth to accommodate the two pieces of glass, two mats and the art. An alternative frame, other than the grooved type described earlier, is to join two frames back-to-back with the entire project sandwiched in between. In this case the rabbet depth must be accurately designed to ensure an exact fit with no slack space. This will safeguard the framing project from dust getting in. A frame of this kind can be glued and nailed. If the frame will need to be taken apart later on, the two frames can be joined with screws inserted into pre-drilled, countersunk holes.

This project may be hung in a window, on a wall or attached to a base for free-standing.

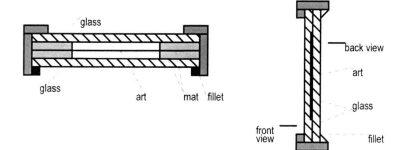

Glass Trap with mats   **Glass Trap without mats**

Object Box Framing

Introduction

Although it has been said that memory is a momentary thing, being a creative, innovative framer will allow you to dispel that idea. Framers who show customers the excitement of taking a significant moment, happening or even a piece of memorabilia and by framing it beautifully and creatively, gain not only appreciative clients but also handsome profits.

The things some people hang in their homes or office walls is difficult to figure out. Having said that, however, just look around. Nothing is too ordinary or too bizarre that it should not be considered creative or imaginative for displaying. I have framed two pieces off the Berlin Wall, a telephone, a screwdriver, dishes, a boy's suit, a violin, and countless other items, each presenting an enjoyable challenge. As time went on I sought out two categories for framing—needlework and three-dimensional items. These became my specialties.

Designing the Object Box

1. Selecting article(s) to be framed:

> Of what significance is this item?
> Are there other articles that go with it?
> The item is probably part of the customer's life.
> Photographs are important.

2. Arrangement of the articles:

> Refrain from the "military rule" – all items in line.
>
> Do not overcrowd.
>
> If colours are a problem, select neutrals.
>
> Fabric covered mats are preferred, except if the object is made of fabric.

Materials for Framing

1. Frame size:

Standard sizes, such as 5"x7" or 8"x10", might be most economical.

Make them large enough to avoid the crowded look.

2. Selecting appropriate framing:

Using pre-made and pre-finished moulding speeds up the framing project.

Suppliers have a wide selection of wood or metal frame mouldings available; making your own is time consuming and in the long run, pricey.

If convex glass must be used to accommodate the depth required, make sure suitable moulding is available.

3. Other materials:

Mounting boards may be made from regular, rag, fabric covered mat board, foam board, or thin plywood.

Fabric covered board may be commercially manufactured or the framer can use almost any fabric and a heat or vacuum press.

Glass/mirror may be used for the back of the object box.

Attaching or Fitting

1. Articles in the frame:

Mighty Mounts - clear plastic, versatile mounting devices.

Silicone; a clear adhesive, must be used with care and in a ventilated area.

Thread - either coloured or clear filament; very reliable, inexpensive, easily reversible.

Velcro.

2. Joining wood mouldings to create a deeper object box:

Use glue and nails in inconspicuous areas for square or rectangular boxes, place nails in the top and bottom, so they may not be seen from the sides; special frames such as circles, ovals and octagons are very attractive for object framing.

3. Glass:

Glazing should be restricted to clear glass, conservation and museum glass and clear acrylic; non-glare type glass should be avoided because the further away it is from the object, the more distortion occurs.

4. Final fitting:

Use either saw-tooth hangers or wire near the top to keep the project from swinging out from the wall; it should hang vertically.

The back may be held in place with turn buttons for easy access, which might be necessary from time to time.

Attach bumper pads to permit air circulation at the back.

Objects for Framing

When many people think of decor for their homes, things like old eye glasses, grandfather's shaving equipment and personal effects do not readily come to mind. Memorabilia can make elegant wall art when consigned to the workmanship of experienced framers. In actual fact there is no limit to the types of objects customers might bring in for processing.

Typical objects are military medals, athletic awards, academic honours, plates, spoons, dolls, dried flowers, clothing, coins, souvenirs, anniversary mementos, guns, knives, buttons, insects, land title deeds, bulletins, schedules, sports memorabilia, pieces of needlework along with needles and crochet hooks.

GLOSSARY

Acid – any of a class of substances that liberate hydrogen ions in water, are usually corrosive and have a pH of less than 7.0.

Acid-Free – a term used to describe any material that is either naturally without acid or that has been neutralized with a buffering agent such as calcium carbonate.

Acid Migration – is the transfer of acid from an acidic material to a less acidic or neutral material.

Acrylic – a plastic noted for transparency, light weight, weather resistance, colour fastness and rigidity, which can be substituted for glass in framing. It is shatter-resistant and can be procured with UV filtering ability. Common trade names are Perspex, Lucite and Plexiglas.

Alkali – are substances having a pH over 7.0 which may be added to material to neutralize acids.

Alkaline Reserve – an added supply of buffering agent that increases the alkalinity of the paper to defend against environmental acids.

Alpha Cellulose – the longest of the cellulose fibres that are the main constituent of all plant life. Alpha cellulose fibres are required for the production of permanent papers because their length and crystalline structure make them the strongest, most stable type of cellulose.

Alum-Rosin – an acidic sizing agent known to accelerate the deterioration of paper.

Annealing – the process of cooling glass slowly and evenly, to eliminate stresses, which build up during manufacture.

Buffering – the process by which an excess of acid neutralizing component is included as an ingredient of paper, and which will offer protection against further deterioration caused by acidity.

Calcium Carbonate – an alkaline chemical used as a buffer, or neutralizer, in paper.

Conservation – a method of mounting and framing a piece of artwork in a preservation manner, including mounting, matting, glazing, framing and fitting.

Cotton Linters – the fibres removed from the cotton seed casing for the manufacture of cotton papers and boards.

Cullet – broken or reject glass collected for recycling.

De-acidification – is a term for a chemical treatment that neutralizes the acid content of paper and deposits an alkaline buffer to counter future acid attack. A more exact term is "neutralization."

Deckle Edge – describes the decorative, uneven, feathered edge of fine-quality papers.

Fallout – is the piece which is removed when a window opening is cut in a mat.

Fillet – a strip of decorative wood or plastic fitted in the mat window opening to enhance the artwork; also to provide spacing between the art and the glass.

Float – to attach an artwork onto a mounting board so that all the edges of the piece can be seen even if a mat is used, in which case the window opening would be greater in size than the artwork.

Float Glass – is brought about by floating molten glass on a bath of molten tin. Float glass is smooth, consistent in density and is the type most frequently selected for picture framing.

Foxing – brown or reddish spots in paper resembling rust stains usually caused by iron salt impurities in the paper coming in contact with condensation behind the glass, or in some cases caused by fungus.

Giclée (zhee-klay) – prints are created typically using professional 8-colour to 12-colour ink jet printers. The term "giclée print" conveys an elevation in printmaking technology. Images are produced from high resolution digital scans and printed with archival quality inks onto various substrates including canvas, fine art, and photo-base paper. The process provides better colour accuracy than other means of reproduction.

Glazing – glass or acrylic sheeting placed between the environment and the artwork.

Ground Wood Pulp – a source of cellulose fibre used in paper manufacturing.

Japanese Paper – long-fibred, acid-free paper (tissue) used for hinging art.

Lignin – an organic substance which acts as a binder for the cellulose fibres in wood and certain plants, adding strength and rigidity to the cell walls. Lignin is undesirable in the production of fine permanent papers because it reacts with light and heat to produce phenols and acids which cause deterioration of the paper.

Linocut – a relief print from a block of linoleum cut in the same manner as a woodcut. The printed surface has less texture than a woodcut because of the consistent nature of linoleum.

Lithography – involves the printing of an image from a flat surface. The technique, which was invented in the late 18th century, relies on the principle that oil and water repel each other. Traditionally employing a limestone slab which has been roughened or smoothed according to the effects desired, the lithographer draws directly on the surface with a greasy crayon or with a brush and a liquid ink called tusche. Drawings for lithographs can also be made on specially treated zinc or aluminum plates—hence zincography and algraphy.

Mat Board – paper board used in the picture framing industry to make mats.

Metric Conversion – to convert length in inches to millimetres (mm) divide by 0.03937; to change area from square feet to square metres, divide the square feet by 10.76.

Mylar™ – a strong, pH neutral, clear 100% synthetic polyester resin film, that is durable, stable with electrical and thermal barrier characteristics.

Offset Lithography – an application of lithographic techniques to commercial and quantity production. An image can be photographed onto a stone, zinc, paper or aluminum plate, by the interjection of a screen. The resulting production can be printed in the usual way by hand inking and hand printing. The printing process can, however, be expedited by the use of an offset printing machine.

Paste – an adhesive preparation usually with water as the medium; pastes most generally used in conservation/preservation work are cooked wheat or rice starch.

pH – a symbol for the degree of acidity or alkalinity of a substance. The range varies from 0 to 14, making 7 neutral and anything below 7 as acidic and anything above 7, alkalinic.

Rabbet (rebate-UK) – the step or recess in a moulding into which all the components of framing project are fitted.

Ruling Pen – is a pen with two parallel, adjustable blades. These are filled with ink or water-colour and used to draw decorative lines on mats.

Sizing – a substance added to paper that fills in spaces between fibres. Sizing allows paper to accept ink, resist water and have greater tear strength, depending on the amount and type of sizing used.

Silkscreen (serigraphy) – the artist stretches a piece of fine silk over a wooden frame and then glues a design in the form of a stencil to the fabric. Paint (or silkscreen ink) is then forced through the screen onto a sheet of paper beneath it by means of a squeegee. The uncovered areas of fabric will, of course, allow the paint to pass through, while the areas covered by the stencil will not. Most current stencils are more sophisticated. These include:

- the sealing of the areas of silk, which are not to be printed, with an adhesive rather than a cut-paper stencil
- a method in which the design is drawn on the screen with lithographic tusche, after which the screen is covered with a thin coating of glue or size and finally washed with benzine, which dissolves the areas of tusche (see lithography) so the paint can pass through the design, but does not dissolve the glue
- the use of light metal rather than fabric screens; and the use of photo-sensitized film as the stencil so that photographic images can be reproduced.

Stretcher Bar – describes a wood frame to which canvas art, usually an oil or acrylic painting is stretched and attached prior to framing.

TAPPI – Technical Association of the Pulp and Paper Industry; an organization dedicated to providing and advancing research and technology within the pulp and paper industry.

Ultraviolet Radiation – lies beyond the violet end of the visible spectrum

United Inches – the sum of two adjacent sides; for example a frame 16" X 20" signifies 36 United Inches (UI).

Woodcut – the artist draws a design directly on a flat block of wood (usually cut on the side grain). Using a gouge or sharp knife, the carver (sometimes, but not necessarily the artist) then cuts away everything but the lines and areas of the image. The design which is to be inked and printed thus stands in relief. The chiaroscuro woodcut is a colour woodcut with a different block for each colour, suggesting the effect of tonal drawing.

See 1stWorld Books at:

www.1stWorldPublishing.com

See our classic collection at:

www.1stWorldLibrary.com

Printed in the United States
140512LV00001B/10/P

9 781421 890012